EVERY MANAGER'S LEGAL GUIDE TO HIRING

EVERY MANAGER'S LEGAL GUIDE TO HIRING

August Bequai

Dow Jones-Irwin
Homewood, Illinois 60430

© RICHARD D. IRWIN, INC., 1990

Dow Jones-Irwin is a trademark of Dow Jones & Company, Inc.

This publication is designed to provide accurate and
authoritative information in regard to the subject matter
covered. It is sold with the understanding that the
publisher is not engaged in rendering legal, accounting, or
other professional service. If legal advice or other expert
assistance is required, the services of a competent
professional person should be sought.

*From a Declaration of Principles jointly adopted by a Committee
of the American Bar Association and a Committee of Publishers.*

Sponsoring editor: Jim Childs
Project editor: Jean Roberts
Production manager: Ann Cassady
Jacket design: Renée Klyczek Nordstrom
Compositor: Bruce Graphics, Inc.
Typeface: 11/13 Century Schoolbook
Printer: R. R. Donnelley & Sons Company

Library of Congress Cataloging-in-Publication Data

Bequai, August.
    Every manager's legal guide to hiring / August Bequai.
        p.   cm.
    Includes index.
    ISBN 1-55623-154-7
    1. Employee selection—Law and legislation—United States.
I. Title.
KF3457.B47   1990
344.73'0125—dc20
[347.304125]   89–34730
                                                                        CIP

Printed in the United States of America

1 2 3 4 5 6 7 8 9 0 DO 6 5 4 3 2 1 0 9

For
Haxhi Bequai
and Samuel Goldman,
both deceased,
who believed in
ethics and professionalism

PREFACE

A few years ago, most employers would have said you were crazy if you told them they ran the risk of being sued every time they interviewed a job applicant. But that's how the American employment process stands today. As an attorney, I know exactly where applicants go when they think a potential employer has discriminated against them.

Personnel law is the great leveler. It doesn't matter whether your company is big or small, whether it's based in a large urban center or a tiny rural hamlet, or whether it produces automobiles or software. No matter what kind of employer you are, you've undoubtedly discovered that the road to hiring qualified employees is full of legal potholes.

Take the case of the electronics plant that denied a female applicant a job as an assembly trainee because she had preschool children. The company's policy toward hiring male trainees was nowhere near as restrictive, so the applicant sued. The judge noted that the company couldn't justify its separate-but-unequal hiring practices for male and female employees with young children, and ruled in the applicant's favor.

Here's another case that's very typical of what's going on in employment law today. A glass factory paid its male packers more than their female counterparts. The company tried to rationalize the difference because the men lifted cartons while the women used hand trucks. But the judge took another view. Under the Federal Equal Pay Act, he said, "equal" does not mean identical. Substantially equal is enough, and minor differences in duties don't warrant major differences in salary.

The 1980s have the dubious honor of being perhaps the most litigious decade in recorded history. The two cases I described represent a tiny fraction of the 500,000-plus that crowd the court and regulatory agency dockets every year.

Litigation may sometimes seem like the only way out of the labyrinth of laws that determine the American employer-employee relationship. But employment law really isn't as arcane as many people think. A good deal of it rests on a foundation of about a dozen acts, including the Equal Employment Opportunity Act, the Civil Rights Act of 1964, the Federal Equal Pay Act, the Federal Rehabilitation Act of 1973, Executive Order 11246, the Age Discrimination in Employment Act, the Immigration Reform and Control Act of 1986, and the Occupational Safety and Health Act.

These are the laws that determine how you:

1. Advertise jobs, whether on bulletin boards or in the media.
2. Establish recruitment procedures.
3. Check out references and professional credentials.
4. Conduct job interviews.
5. Maintain records on applicants and new employees.
6. Communicate with employment agencies.
7. Test for AIDS and other diseases.
8. Administer drug and alcohol tests.
9. Frame the questions you ask applicants.

Many books have been written about the American employment scene, but few have zeroed in on hiring. The few books on hiring law that I've run across are loaded with deadly jargon that makes no sense unless you have a J.D. degree. This book is different: It takes a nontechnical approach to its subject, with the emphasis on real-life applications and solutions rather than theoretical analysis. At the end of each chapter, you'll find one or more "rules to hire by" that encapsulate the chapter's message.

This book tells supervisors, executives, personnel directors, personnel managers and other human resource personnel, and anyone else who makes hiring decisions in an organization what they need to know about the law of hiring.

It begins with a review of the employment-at-will doctrine, which still has a profound effect on how we hire and fire in America. After a discussion on job applicants' privacy rights, I look at the laws affecting how employers recruit, screen, test, and interview applicants in their never ending quest to find the best person for the job. Throughout the book, my emphasis is on how to do these things without getting into legal trouble.

Few employers understand how the Equal Employment Opportunity Commission (EEOC), the U.S. Department of Labor, and other regulatory agencies operate, so I've provided an inside look at what the key regulators do and how they influence just about every phase of hiring.

In hiring law, discrimination is the watchword. Obviously, no book on this subject would be complete without a discussion of how to defend yourself against discrimination charges, so I've given you some solid defensive strategies that you can apply every day. There's also a discussion of affirmative-action programs that you, your workers, and the EEOC can live with.

The book finishes with employment contracts and record-keeping requirements for employers.

I wrote this book to help you stay out of the courthouse as you choose the best-qualified workers for your company. I see the book as a sort of primer; I think it will be most valuable to personnel managers with little experience in hiring law. But it should also provide a quick refresher for the busy employer with more legal knowledge.

While new laws that affect hiring are made every day, the fundamentals of hiring law haven't changed that much. I hope *Every Manager's Legal Guide to Hiring* will help you understand those fundamentals a little better.

ACKNOWLEDGMENTS

I wish to thank Carmen D. Wiseman for editing and preparing the manuscript for publication, Dolores Heidenthal for typing the manuscript, and my wife, Mary Ryan Bequai, for her ongoing help and support.

August Bequai

CONTENTS

Testing   Discrimination   Business Environment   Where the Law
Stands   *Drug Testing   Alcohol Testing   Contagious Diseases   Lie-
Detector Tests   Honesty Tests   Psychological Tests   Genetic
Screening*   Testing Tips

Employment Act   Title VII   *Discrimination Charges*   Government
Contractors   *Public Contracts Act   Service Contract Act   Apprentices
and Trainees*   Disclosing Personnel Records   *How to Get into
Trouble   Protecting Yourself*

CHAPTER 1

HIRING AND THE LAW

Until the 1930s, American employers ran their businesses as if they were medieval kingdoms. Employers had the power of feudal lords, and employees weren't much better off than serfs: They could be taken on, chewed up, and disposed of at the boss's whim. Basically, workers left their constitutional rights at the factory or office door.

It took a generation of labor unrest, but things did change. In fact, workers now have so many rights, especially during the preemployment period, that the scales of justice appear to have tipped in their favor:

• In Los Angeles, a job seeker in his 50s takes a computer company to court for age discrimination, claiming that the company has systematically bypassed older job applicants in favor of younger ones. The jury finds the company guilty and awards the man $500,000 in damages.

• A group of female job applicants sues a Connecticut grocery chain for sex discrimination. They state that the company rejected them because they didn't meet its height and weight requirements even though those requirements had no bearing on jobs they were applying for. The grocery chain eventually settles out of court for $4 million.

• Several Muslims charge a New York telecommunications company with discriminatory hiring practices because a personnel interviewer had told them they could not take time off for Muslim holidays even though members of other faiths got time off for their holidays. The Muslim applicants win the suit. (This company just doesn't know how to stay out of hot water: The U.S. Department of Justice has also investigated it for allegedly violating the antidiscrimination provisions of the Immigration Reform and Control Act of 1986.)

Congress, the courts, and many local legislative bodies have all placed limits on what employers can and can't do in hiring. The result is a crazy quilt of laws and ordinances, sometimes contradictory and almost always confusing. For instance, honesty or "attitude" tests, while perfectly legal in Delaware and Georgia, are severely restricted in Rhode Island and Massachusetts.

Then there's the AIDS pandemic, which the law hasn't made up its mind about yet. At this writing, San Francisco, Houston, and Los Angeles ban AIDS testing at the preemployment stage, but many cities do not have such a prohibition.

Employers who don't stay within the letter of the often-confusing law in hiring may face an endless, draining round of lawsuits. But that's not all employers have to worry about these days: They're also duty-bound to ensure that the people they hire don't threaten anyone's health and safety, whether their own or that of their co-workers and other innocent persons. Failure to identify potentially dangerous individuals is another surefire ticket to court, as these recent cases demonstrate:

• A woman sued a hotel chain for $1 million because one of the hotel's employees attacked her while she was sleeping in her room. When the police arrested the employee, they learned that he had a criminal record; in fact, he'd made a similar attack on a female guest while working for another hotel. Attorneys advised the hotel chain to settle the case out of court.

• A computer company was sued because one of its clients accused a company employee of infecting the client's machines with a "virus." In researching the case, the client's lawyers learned that the employee had a history of hacking. The company would have discovered the same thing if it had thoroughly checked his references. Faced with exposure of its slipshod personnel practices, the company chose to settle out of court.

• Alleging that a physician at a large city hospital had made sexual advances to her, a female patient sued the hospital for $15 million. When the hospital checked into the allegation, it learned not only that the doctor had been fired by another hospital for similar misconduct, but that he'd fabricated his medical credentials! The hospital's insurance company is trying to negotiate a settlement with the woman.

American employers should screen would-be employees to weed out potential safety risks to others—but they must also screen to protect their own assets. Employee theft and misuse of property account for huge losses each year. According to the U.S. Department of Justice, unscrupulous employees steal more than $20 billion annually from their employers. And the U.S. Chamber of Commerce attributes 50 percent of business failures in the United States each year to employee dishonesty.

If you think this is all penny-ante thievery committed by workers at the lowest rungs of the corporate ladder, guess again. The American Bar Association has warned that the cost of some computer crimes might run as high as $10 million per incident, and that unethical corporate insiders will probably be behind many of these episodes. Also, a study by the American Institute of Public Accountants has found that employees in high-trust positions commit the bulk of financial thefts.

What does all this mean to you, the employer or personnel manager? Obviously, you must tread cautiously. At the very least, you must make sure your hiring practices don't violate any federal or local laws. But what else can you do to avoid a lawsuit or an investigation by the Equal Employment Opportunity Commission (EEOC)? Is it possible to keep prospective employees, labor unions, and consumer activist groups happy and still protect your interests? Yes—as long as you *hire right.*

What hiring right takes is an understanding of how the employment process works from day to day. In this book, I'll explain the rules and regulations that shape the current employment scene and how they affect hiring. My goal is not to turn you into a lawyer but to tell you how to keep the lawyers off your back, because hiring-related litigation does nothing but hurt the bottom line and divert valuable resources from your organization.

TODAY'S EMPLOYMENT–AT–WILL DOCTRINE

Throughout much of the 19th century, it was taken for granted in American law that without a specific contractual arrangement, an employer could hire or fire "at will"—for good reason, bad reason, or no reason at all. The other side of the at-will coin was that employees could work for whom they pleased and for as long as they wanted.

The American employment-at-will doctrine, a product of several centuries of customary or "common" law, survived almost intact into the early 1930s. Then came the New Deal's prolabor legislative agenda to alter the American employment process forever. Employers could no longer hire and fire capriciously. Moreover, workers could take complaints against their employers to the courts or government regulatory agencies, which could impose both civil and criminal penalties.

Actually, there's still an employment-at-will doctrine, though it has very little in common with the old doctrine outside of its name. The New Deal may have killed off the original at-will doctrine, but the Great Society and the reforms of the 1970s and 1980s revived it long enough to give it a major facelift.

This revised employment-at-will doctrine remains the foundation of the American employer-employee relationship. Many courts continue to pay lip service to it; in fact, some states pride themselves on being at-will jurisdictions. Die-hard proponents of the free enterprise system believe that capitalism would wither without it. And constitutional purists view the doctrine as embodying the essence of the 13th Amendment, which ended slavery in the United States.

The only trouble with the revised at-will doctrine is that it's like a Monopoly game with countless rules and regulations that can easily land employers in "jail." Because the federal and state governments churn out thousands of laws every day, keeping up with the revised doctrine's ins and outs can be a nightmare.

To make life even harder for employers who want to do the right thing by prospective employees, the courts, Congress, and federal regulatory agencies have all carved out *exceptions* to the revised at-will doctrine over the years. Even lawyers find all these laws and exceptions mind-boggling . . . so how are employers and personnel managers expected to deal with them?

The Courts Take Exception

Fortunately, it's possible to identify general trends in judicial thinking on the at-will exceptions. If you know what the courts are up to, the at-will doctrine is a lot less likely to trip you up.

Fairness and Equity
These principles lie at the heart of the U.S. legal system, and the courts have made it clear that they apply to the hiring process, too. You can still hire at will, but the worker's race, ethnic background, sex, political affiliation, or religious preference cannot enter into the hiring decision.

Public Policy
The courts have also determined that hiring practices can't fly in the face of established social precepts and mores. For instance, you can't refuse to hire a worker who has been selected to serve on a jury because jury service is too deeply engrained in our public culture. Judges, of all people, can appreciate what would happen to the jury system if employers were allowed to thumb their noses at it.

An essential part of the judicial stance on public-policy exceptions to the at-will doctrine is the feeling that employees can't be penalized if they don't go along with an employer's unlawful acts. Company loyalty doesn't extend to, say, committing perjury to shield a boss who commits a crime.

Likewise, you can't refuse to hire a worker who has blown the whistle on a former employer's crimes—or, for that matter, any person who gives testimony about a company's wrongdoing in a trial or administrative hearing. (Michigan and a few other states even have "whistle-blower" laws on the books to prevent retaliation by employers.) The courts believe, rightly, that refusing to hire such "troublemakers" would undermine our legal system.

The courts also won't tolerate discrimination in hiring against anyone who has filed a suit or complaint against a former employer. Recently, a New Jersey boss got into trouble when he refused to hire a female applicant who had filed an EEOC complaint against her previous employer.

Many jurists have stated that employers can't discriminate against pro-union job applicants. The California courts, for example, have consistently ruled against employers who refuse to hire applicants with union backgrounds. The courts also frown on refusal to hire applicants who have filed for workers' compensation.

Now, this doesn't mean you have to hire unqualified applicants because they might use public-policy exceptions to the at-will doctrine as grounds for legal action. An applicant can't hold a public-policy gun to a prospective employer's head. You should hire only people who have the skills, training, and professional outlook to do the job—that's all the revised at-will doctrine asks. On the other hand, an employer who blacklists or retaliates against an individual who follows the dictates of public policy is asking for a lawsuit.

Good Faith

Some courts have established a "good faith" exception to the at-will doctrine. As far as these judges are concerned, employment-at-will that is motivated by an employer's "bad faith" (dishonest or malicious behavior) is not in the best interests of the U.S. economic system. That's because the employment relationship is like any other contractual bond: Both sides must be fair and above-board in their dealings with each other.

The good-faith exception ensures that employers won't gain anything from misrepresentations, fraudulent statements, or unethical behavior toward prospective employees. And it gives applicants something to fall back on if public policy doesn't apply and there's no written employment agreement.

Implied Contracts

The courts are often willing to set the at-will doctrine aside if an employee can demonstrate the existence of an "implied contract" with his or her employer. If an employer promises an applicant a job and the applicant accepts, the two have an implied contract—and the applicant can make the employer honor it, as these two examples show:

• In a recent Michigan case, an employer dangled a wonderful job with a high salary and great benefits before a man who worked for a competitive company. Seduced by the prospective employer's promises, the man wasted no time in quitting his job with the competitor. Unfortunately, the employer reneged on his promises, so the applicant sued him. The judge observed that the employer's statements created a contract and decided the suit in favor of the applicant.

• A California firm induced an executive to leave his job in New York and move to the West Coast. When the executive arrived in California, however, he found that the promised position had been filled by someone else. "Sorry, " said the employer. "We gave it to the best man." The judge disagreed, and the executive won.

Promissory Estoppel

Closely allied with the implied-contract exception is the legal concept of "promissory estoppel." This is a fancy term for making employers keep their fabulous promises to applicants. Thus, if an employer promises job security to a prospective employee in an attempt to obtain a long-standing commitment, the employer must honor that promise. Otherwise, as the courts have ruled, there would be a serious injustice.

A growing number of judges are ruling in favor of employees who can demonstrate that they believed and were hurt by a prospective employer's pie-in-the-sky promises of job security and higher pay. Promissory estoppel, if successfully wielded, is a double-edged sword for employers: Not only must they follow through on their promises, but employees can sue them for losses and damages if they don't.

At-Will on Trial

Over the past decade, the courts have chipped away at the at-will doctrine to such an extent that anything predating 1988 in this area of employment law is considered the "old" at-will doctrine. Erosion has been especially severe in Massachusetts, California, New York, Michigan, and Illinois (Table 1–1). It's almost reached the point where the exceptions have become the rule.

In real-life terms, this means an applicant may try to sue you under one of the at-will exceptions. Of course, the case may never come near a courtroom. Judges get annoyed when employers fail to

TABLE 1–1
At-Will Exceptions in the United States

Exception	States Where Applicable
Statements from personnel managers are as binding as a written contract.	Alabama, Alaska, Arizona, California, District of Columbia, Florida, Idaho, Illinois, Indiana, Maine, Michigan, Minnesota, Nevada, New Mexico, New York, Ohio, Oregon, Pennsylvania, South Dakota, Washington
Employer can be sued for bad faith.	Alaska, California, Connecticut, Massachusetts, Nevada, New Hampshire
Employer can be sued for not hiring because of applicant's political beliefs or refusal to violate laws.	Arizona, Arkansas, California, Colorado, Connecticut, District of Columbia (political beliefs, by statute), Florida, Hawaii, Idaho, Illinois, Indiana, Kansas, Maryland, Michigan, Missouri, Montana, New Hampshire, Nevada, New Jersey, New Mexico, Oregon, Pennsylvania, Tennessee (statute), Texas, Washington, West Virginia, Wisconsin
Employer can be sued for not hiring whistle-blowers.	Idaho, Illinois, Michigan, Montana, New Hampshire

reach out-of-court agreements with employees because the courts would rather devote their limited resources to more urgent litigation.

If there is a trial, the judge may favor passing the case on to a jury—and juries tend to side with applicants, especially in large urban centers. The judge or jury may also decide in favor of a would-be employee if the local job market is in bad shape.

But the outcome of hiring-related trials is often unpredictable because it depends on so many variables. The court looks at the *totality* of the preemployment relationship in a hiring dispute. That means all pertinent materials, including correspondence between employer and applicant, job advertisements, and so on. What's there certainly can sway the verdict in one direction or the other.

Recruitment procedures come under close scrutiny in hiring cases, too. If a manager steps over the line in describing a position to a prospective employee, that manager may be liable under the law as well as his or her company.

When it looks as if an employer has behaved outrageously or acted in bad faith, the court will almost always try to make some sort of restitution to the employee. In "pain and suffering" cases, for instance, the employer may have to pay heavy punitive damages.

The Government Steps In

Federal and state laws give the judicial exceptions to the at-will doctrine extra clout. Even if employers can skirt a judicial at-will exception, they'll eventually get caught in the statutory net.

Over the last 40 years, the U.S. Congress has dramatically increased regulation of the hiring process. This effort, which encompasses the 1964 Civil Rights Act and other crucial pieces of legislation, has had three primary aims: to prohibit hiring and firing of employees because of age, race, sex, national origin, and other "status" factors; to prohibit discrimination in hiring against employees who simply exercise their legal rights; and to prohibit discrimination in hiring against individuals who file a legitimate grievance with a federal agency.

Civil Rights Act of 1964

Although some conservative members of Congress have tried to water it down, the Civil Rights Act of 1964 is still the most important federal vehicle for fighting discrimination on almost every front.

Title VII of the Civil Rights Act specifically forbids discrimination in employment based on race, religion, or national origin. Exceptions to Title VII coverage include homosexuals, drug or alcohol abusers, and foreign nationals.

The act itself doesn't say much about sex discrimination. But EEOC guidelines hold that it's a violation of Title VII to refuse to hire an applicant because of sexual stereotyping or the preferences of co-workers, clients, or customers. Likewise, employers can't label jobs as "men's" or "women's" positions in help-wanted ads unless sex is a bona fide occupational qualification for the job.

Some antiquated state and local labor laws restrict the employment of women in mining, law enforcement, and other hazardous occupations. The EEOC position is that Title VII supersedes these laws, so they can't be used as grounds for refusing to hire otherwise qualified female applicants.

A 1978 amendment to the act prohibits employers from discriminating on the basis of "medical condition." So far, the courts have interpreted this to mean pregnancy and childbirth; efforts to include cancer patients have run aground.

The Civil Rights Act of 1964 applies to all domestic and foreign concerns doing business in the United States—corporations, partnerships, unions, employment agencies, and multinationals. Title VII applies to employers with 15 or more employees, as well as to labor unions with 15 or more members and joint labor-management committees for apprenticeship and training.

As employers, American Indian tribes are exempt from the act because they are self-governing entities. Religious institutions are naturally free to hire members of their own faith, but that doesn't mean they can discriminate on the basis of race, sex, color, or national origin.

Enforcement of Title VII rests with both the EEOC and the people who have been discriminated against. Section 704(a) of Title VII makes it illegal to discriminate against prospective employees who assist, testify, or participate in investigations, proceedings, or hearings under the act.

Executive Order 11246
This order prevents federal contractors and subcontractors, or individuals with federal or federally assisted construction contracts of $10,000 or more, from discriminating against applicants because of sex, race, color, religion, or national origin. Employers affected by the order must take affirmative action in recruitment, job advertisements, hiring, termination, pay rates, and selection for apprenticeship and training.

The order applies to *all* of a federal contractor's facilities, even if they're not involved in carrying out the federal contract. When a local government holds a federal contract, however, only the participating government agency must comply—with the exception of medical and educational institutions.

The Office of Federal Contract Compliance Programs (OFCCP), a branch of the U.S. Department of Labor, enforces Executive Order 11246. The OFCCP sets policy and develops regulations for implementing the order, and checks to see that federal contractors live up to its standards. Compliance reviews are its primary mechanism for carrying out the government's goal of furthering equal employment opportunity.

The OFCCP has a fairly wide-ranging set of sex-discrimination guidelines, which should be of particular interest to employers working on construction projects. Among other things, the guidelines state that federal contractors may not advertise for "male" and "female" jobs, deny a person a job because of state "protective" labor laws, or make distinctions between married or unmarried persons of only one sex.

Federal Rehabilitation Act of 1973

This act protects individuals with disabilities from discrimination if they work for the federal government or for organizations that hold federal contracts, or if they participate in programs or activities that receive federal funds.

Under amended section 503 of the act, federal contractors and subcontractors with contracts greater than $2,500 cannot discriminate against someone with a physical or mental disability if that person is otherwise qualified to do the job. This section covers hiring, firing, promotions, and compensation.

The OFCCP is also responsible for enforcing section 503. OFCCP regulations on affirmative action for federal contractors and subcontractors call for outreach and positive recruitment of workers with disabilities. Contractors must also make an effort to accommodate an applicant's physical limitations.

The OFCCP enforcement process includes investigation, conciliation, and occasional litigation. If a contractor loses a section 503 suit, the government may withhold payment for the job and bar him or her from future federal contracts.

Section 504 of the act, amended in 1978, forbids discrimination against handicapped individuals in programs or activities receiving federal funds. Various courts have held that this section allows individuals to take legal action against such programs for discrimination. Nonetheless, only the agency providing the federal funds can actually enforce section 504.

There are also many state fair-employment laws that forbid discrimination against workers with disabilities. State departments of labor and state human rights commissions are responsible for enforcing these laws.

Age Discrimination in Employment Act

Now that the huge cohort of postwar baby boomers is getting older, a lot of American employees are going to be thankful for the Age Discrimination in Employment Act of 1967, which prohibits discrimination against employees between 40 and 70 years old. (There is no upper age limit for federal government employees.) The act applies to both public and private companies with 20 or more employees, to employment agencies serving covered employers, and to labor unions with 25 or more members.

Under the act, employers are prohibited from running help-wanted advertisements that indicate preferences, limitations, specifications, or any other form of discrimination based on age. Thus, an employer cannot ask for a "girl" to fill a position (the employer who does so is probably bucking for a sex-discrimination suit anyway) or stipulate that only applicants between the ages of 30 and 35 apply. Of course, the law does allow employers to discipline or fire older employees for dishonesty, poor performance, and other "good cause" reasons.

In some jobs, such as modeling "junior miss" fashions, age is a genuine occupational qualification. The act does not apply to those jobs or to situations in which hiring differences are based on reasonable factors other than age. It's perfectly all right, for instance, to have prospective employees undergo physical examinations if the job makes heavy physical demands on those who perform it. Bona fide seniority systems, as well as retirement, pension, and insurance plans, are also acceptable. But the act does forbid using employee benefit plans as grounds for not hiring older applicants.

To bolster the federal act's safeguards, many states have enacted age discrimination laws or included provisions in their fair employment practices laws that ban discrimination based on age. Some of these state laws place no cap on protection against age discrimination in employment; others protect workers until they reach 60, 65, or 70 years of age.

DON'T GET STUNG BY AT-WILL

Now that you know the legal potholes of the revised at-will doctrine, it should be fairly easy to avoid them. Here are some preemployment guidelines that can help.

Sensible Promises

Never make verbal or written promises that you're not prepared to honor. I'm not saying that an employer cannot give a sales pitch to a prospective employee about how great the job is or how many doors it will open. The courts accept that sales pitches are part of the employment game. But a sales pitch doesn't include promises that you have no means (or intention) of keeping.

If you do promise anything to a prospective employee, make sure it's a reasonable promise. Weigh the risk of losing the employee to a competitor against the probability of a lawsuit if the employee comes on board and learns that your preemployment promises are fairy tales. Be forthright about the applicant's chances for advancement or success, and tell him or her the bad as well as the good points of the job. (Obviously, there's nothing to stop you from emphasizing the good points!)

Civilized Behavior

You might be tempted not to hire a prospective employee because that person has been involved in a lawsuit, administrative action, or complaint against a previous employer—but the satisfaction of retaliating against such a "troublemaker" isn't worth the legal hassle. And don't even think of refusing to hire an applicant for serving on a jury, testifying on behalf of a co-worker, or being active in a labor union.

The boss of a Soviet collective might use blacklisting and coercion to keep a worker from being hired. The boss of a law-abiding American company should avoid such tactics at all costs.

Straight Talk

From the start, let the applicant know what the acceptable standards of behavior are for the job. This simple precaution should defuse most litigation under the exceptions to the at-will doctrine.

Always be candid with prospective employees, and tell them what's required if they want the job. If the applicant must undergo a physical examination or psychological evaluation, for instance, let him or her know right away. Failure to be up-front about prickly issues such as testing can lead to charges of discrimination; the courts may think you're trying to single out a particular group in the work force for a certain test.

If the job has a probationary period, inform the applicant *before* he or she comes on board. Springing this information on an employee after he or she is hired could be construed as an act of bad faith. Also, be sure to tell all prospective employees that reductions in the company's work force, or the closing of a branch or department, might be grounds for withdrawing a job offer.

Of course, you want straight talk from prospective employees, too, so during your interviews, make it clear to applicants that false statements or omissions in their job applications will be grounds for dismissal if they are hired.

Written Policies

If you plan to hire an applicant, give him or her your corporate policy guidelines, personnel manuals, company handbook, and so on. These materials will detail the conditions of employment and bind the employee to them. It doesn't matter whether the employee actually reads them; by receiving them, he or she acknowledges acceptance of your conditions of employment.

When preparing your employment materials, keep these things in mind:

1. Delete all references to "permanent status" in your employment materials. Instead, use terms such as *regular employees* or *full-time employees*. This gives you the flexibility to dismiss employees who don't perform as expected, and also protects you against the appearance of improper or discriminatory conduct.
2. Consider inserting disclaimers in any job application forms, manuals, or other materials you give prospective employees. A sample disclaimer may state, "From time to time, our company changes its policies and procedures. Existing policies and benefits may have to be reduced or eliminated." Admittedly, disclaimers aren't foolproof, but they can certainly help if a prospective employee sues under an exception to the at-will doctrine.

3. Make sure the employment agreement specifies reasons for termination of employment, as well as procedures for resolving disputes (e.g., use of professional arbitration).

Of course, you should periodically review your employment applications, job interview procedures, and employee handbooks and manuals to make sure that they're in line with the latest rulings from the courts and Congress. Try to stay on top of all relevant legal developments in hiring, both judicial and statutory.

Fair Hiring

Ensure that your hiring practices are uniform and applied equitably—in other words, that they don't appear to favor one group of workers over another. Watch out for "protected groups, " particularly in white-collar employment situations where race, sex, and age discrimination complaints are common. And, of course, promptly communicate all changes in company employment policies and procedures to the people who make hiring decisions.

Ignorance, rather than malevolence, is often at the root of much hiring-related litigation. Unfortunately, there's no such thing as ignorance under the law. But there's also no denying that the law sometimes sends out crossed signals.

Want a "quick fix" to help you stay out of hiring trouble? Just apply the following rule of thumb in all your preemployment activities:

Avoid anything that smacks of bias.

And here are some corollaries to the rule:

- Never appear to prefer one group over another.
- Never pressure prospective employees to mold their political or religious beliefs to your own.
- Never do anything to indicate that hiring or firing decisions might stem from bias.
- Never condone or tolerate discriminatory actions by personnel managers and staff.

All that the new at-will doctrine really asks of employers is that they base their hiring decisions on merit and qualifications for the job. Hold that thought, and you'll be well on the way to understanding the rules of the hiring game.

CHAPTER 2

THE APPLICANT'S RIGHT TO PRIVACY

If you're like the respondents to a survey conducted by the Administrative Management Society, you value work experience, educational background, motivation, and loyalty above all else in your prospective employees. The job market has become so competitive, however, that some applicants embroider their credentials. The last thing you need is an employee who can't do the job because that person isn't what he or she claims to be. But neither do you need a lawsuit for infringing on an applicant's privacy during a routine work history check.

That might sound a bit farfetched. After all, doesn't an employer have the right to confirm whether an applicant really holds an MBA from Harvard or was the president of XYZ Multinational in the past? Yes—up to a point:

• A doctor who had done his residency in a California university hospital applied for staff privileges at several Colorado hospitals. One of them asked his California supervisor for a reference. The supervisor wrote back that the doctor had "performed well below average." As a result, he was denied privileges at the Colorado hospital. He eventually sued both his former supervisor and the hospital that turned him down.

• A man seeking a management position with an Oregon firm gave his previous boss as a reference. The boss wrote the Oregon company that the applicant "was constantly drunk on the job." The man sued the boss, claiming that the letter he sent the company was inaccurate and misleading. The court must have thought so, too—it awarded the man $350,000 in damages.

• An MBA graduate applied for a job with a New York insurance company. During his interview, he said he had graduated in the top 5 percent of his class. To obtain the applicant's actual grade point average, an employee of the insurance company called the applicant's college and pretended to be the applicant. After the applicant had been turned down for the position, he sued the company for invading the privacy of his school records.

Privacy laws and regulations have made the seemingly mundane business of checking out an applicant's credentials much more complicated and dangerous than it used to be. Only a few years ago, employee privacy cases rarely went to trial. When employers run afoul of privacy laws nowadays, however, they often have to pick up a very big tab—the average privacy damage award is a whopping $300,000-plus.

The Institute for the Future recently reported that privacy in the workplace might become the most important employment-related social issue of the 1990s. Whether or not that happens, you're going to need to know more about the privacy rights of prospective employees.

PRIVACY IN AMERICAN LAW

The right to privacy is a relatively recent development in our legal system. Contrary to popular belief, the U.S. Constitution explicitly protects individual privacy only against incursions by the government.

In 1890, Boston law partners Louis Brandeis (a future chief justice of the U.S. Supreme Court) and Samuel S. Warren published an article on the right to privacy. This right, they argued, was implied in past Supreme Court decisions and should be openly recognized as well. The authors were concerned mainly about outrageous newspaper articles about Warren's socialite wife that didn't seem to fall under existing libel law.

Brandeis and Warren noted that defamation of character, including libel and slander, had long been a part of the common law. In defamation cases, however, the plaintiff had to demonstrate injury to his or her *character and reputation*. In invasion-of-privacy cases, the goal was to protect the individual's *feelings*.

Today, the courts widely acknowledge that the privacy of every American is protected by both common and statutory law.

Common-Law Basics

During the preemployment stage, applicants have common-law privacy rights in three key areas: the right not to be portrayed in a false or misleading way, the right to prevent public disclosure of private facts, and the right to be free from unwarranted intrusion. Chief Justice Brandeis said that all of us have the right to be left alone—and that goes for prospective employees, too.

The first of these rights has been the easiest for the courts to apply, mainly because the ancient and inviolable concept of private property lies at its core. In other words, an individual's name and personal information "belong" to that individual; no one can give these things out or alter them in any way without the individual's permission.

The courts recognize that job applicants have the common-law right to sue employers who give out false or misleading information about them. The employer's ignorance of the applicant's privacy rights is no excuse, and punitive damages are a certainty if the applicant can prove that the employer had a grudge against the applicant or otherwise acted maliciously in giving out the false information. The same goes for personnel agencies or others acting in the employer's name.

To win this kind of privacy violation suit, an applicant needs to show only that the employer released information about him or her without permission, that the information was false, and that he or she lost money or suffered as a result.

The common law of privacy also protects job applicants and other employees from unauthorized disclosure of personnel files, college transcripts, and other private facts about themselves. In fact, this facet of the law covers just about every sensitive personal record you can think of. If a prospective employer asks for this kind of information about one of your former employees, keep a lid on it unless the applicant allows you to give it out!

Prospective employees have it even easier in suits involving unauthorized disclosure than in those involving dissemination of false information. All they need to show is that the employer re-

leased private information without the applicant's permission, resulting in financial loss, embarrassment, or "pain and suffering."

Finally, applicants can sue employers for gaining access to
their personnel files and school records without their explicit permission, an offshoot of the common-law right of freedom from unwarranted intrusion into an individual's private affairs.

If you think the common law doesn't mean as much as "real"
statutory laws, keep in mind that the common-law privacy safeguards have become statutory law in many states.

Constitutional Guarantees

Although the U.S. Constitution doesn't mention the right to privacy in so many words, the courts have long accepted that the
Fourth Amendment guarantees such a right. Chief Justice Brandeis, that ever-vigilant champion of privacy rights, believed any
unjustifiable intrusion by the government on individual privacy
was a violation of such Fourth Amendment principles as protection against unreasonable search and seizure.

Most of the cases dealing with constitutional privacy protection have involved intrusion by the government, but the courts are
beginning to widen the circle to encompass the private sector.
Some judges, for instance, have ruled that drug testing violates
constitutional privacy guarantees.

California and a few other states have already incorporated
privacy provisions into their state constitutions, and prospective
employees can use these provisions to prevent employers from mis-
using personnel information and drug test results. This seems to
be the wave of the future, so make sure your preemployment practices are in line with pertinent state constitutional privacy
restrictions.

STATUTORY PRIVACY

Along with common-law and constitutional privacy constraints,
employers must deal with a raft of state and federal laws that determine what kind of information (and how much of it) they can
gain access to in screening job applicants.

Federal Records

Federal agencies collect, store, and disseminate an astonishing amount of personal information on nearly everyone in the United States. To protect the privacy of this information, Congress passed the Federal Privacy Act in 1974.

The act states that, with a few exceptions, government agencies must obtain written permission from an individual before they release any information about him or her. The agency must also record the date, purpose, and person to whom the information was disclosed—and must give the individual this accounting record if he or she asks for it.

For many employers, the Privacy Act may seem like just another roadblock to effective screening of prospective employees: The statute makes it illegal for an employer to access an applicant's federal records without (you guessed it) the applicant's written consent. Employers who try to get around applicants to obtain federal records are likely setting themselves up for federal prosecution.

If you really need to examine an applicant's federal records, however, you can call on the Freedom of Information Act (FOIA), which makes federal records more accessible to the American people. It's the same statute that gives applicants and other members of the public the right to review their government files.

Simply by placing an FOIA request, you can gain access to a surprising number of government files, including an applicant's criminal conviction records and even personal records, such as registration and license applications. Among the few federal records you won't be able to gain access to are personnel and medical files. Also, the government can't give out any information that would obviously violate common-law, statutory, and constitutional guarantees of individual privacy.

Federal agencies *must* provide an employer with their records on an applicant unless they can clearly show that this would be an unwarranted intrusion on the applicant's privacy. The courts have interpreted "unwarranted intrusion" to mean disclosure that would cause more harm than good.

So, the FOIA can be a valuable tool for employers who want to gain access to a job applicant's federal records, as long as the records aren't protected by some federal law. If that happens, the agency that holds the records must prove that they're protected.

Thanks to the Privacy Act and the FOIA, we can all look at our personal government files. But some Americans who've taken advantage of this privilege have been shocked by the errors their records contain.

Basically, it's up to us to do anything about erroneous information in our federal records. Thus, if there are problems with a job applicant's file, the applicant can ask the agency to make corrections—and can then take the agency to court if it refuses to amend the records. In situations where an applicant claims something is wrong with the records and the agency balks at changing them, the applicant can at least demand to have his or her objections noted in any subsequent disclosures of the information.

Criminal History Records

The largest repository of criminal records in the United States is the FBI's Identification Division. Interestingly, more than half of the requests the division receives for criminal record information come not from the police, but from private-sector businesses trying to check out job applicants.

The FBI strictly controls access to these records by private employers. For instance, the Identification Division cannot give out information on arrests that don't result in prosecution within one year, unless the employer is a Department of Defense contractor or in a regulated industry such as banking, securities, or nuclear energy.

Prospective employees have the right to review any criminal history information the FBI maintains on them. Under the Federal Privacy Act, an applicant can request and obtain a copy of his or her FBI records to verify their accuracy. If the applicant shows that the records contain errors, the FBI must review them and make all necessary changes—and if any information needs to be corrected or updated, the FBI must notify every other criminal justice agency in the country. Watch out, though: The FBI doesn't have to notify the private-sector employer who originally requested the information.

In most states, an employer cannot ask applicants about juvenile crime records, arrests that didn't result in convictions, or misdemeanor convictions more than five years old—as long as the applicant has had no other convictions in the meantime. Of course, if you're really keen on unmasking a suspected criminal, you're free to pore over federal and local court records, which are open to the public. Juvenile court records, however, remain sealed.

Credit and Financial Records

Many employers view credit bureaus and private investigative agencies as treasure troves of data on potential employees. No wonder, considering how much information credit bureaus manage to accumulate about one's credit history, work background, and even personal life.

There may be a Big Brother aspect to credit reporting agencies, but the government does regulate the kind of information they can collect, how long they can keep it on file, and whom they can disseminate it to.

For instance, the Fair Credit Reporting Act regulates investigative consumer reports, which employers often use to screen job applicants. To compile these exhaustive reports, the agency interviews neighbors, former employers, acquaintances, and others to dig up information on an individual's personal habits and ethics.

If you want to examine a consumer report on an applicant, the agency that compiled the report must tell the applicant about your request and how much of the record you want to examine. As always, it's a good idea for you to get the applicant's consent for release of these records first.

The Fair Credit Reporting Act limits the period for maintaining most credit records to no longer than seven years. Bankruptcy information is an exception: It can be maintained for 14 years.

It's possible that information in a credit report might cost an applicant a job with your company. If that happens, you must supply the applicant with the name and address of the agency that prepared the report. On request, the agency has to reveal the contents of the report to the applicant. But if the credit records are inaccurate, the applicant can ask the agency to correct them and tell you about the amended report.

The Fair Credit Reporting Act doesn't give employees unlimited access to the information in their credit records, though. An applicant can't just barge into a credit bureau and demand to see or copy his or her files. Likewise, the agency doesn't have to tell the applicant where it got the information in the report.

Several other federal laws limit your right to examine a prospective employee's financial records:

Right to Financial Privacy Act. Armed with subpoenas and search warrants, law enforcement officials can obtain an individual's financial records from a bank, credit card company, or brokerage house under this act. But private employers cannot access such records without written authorization from job applicants.

Electronic Funds Transfer Act. More and more financial transactions are moving through electronic funds transfer (EFT) systems. The Electronic Funds Transfer Act declares that records of EFT transactions are private and confidential, and that employers need a job applicant's written authorization to examine them.

Equal Credit Opportunity Act. This act requires financial institutions to update their records and transactions as necessary and to respect the confidentiality of those records.

There are many federal and state laws designed to protect financial privacy, too many to list here. It's enough to say that they permit you to look at some financial records for the legitimate purpose of screening employees. But certain information, such as bank account records, is strictly off-limits unless the prospective employee voluntarily gives you permission to see it. And you certainly can't force employees to give such authorization as a condition for employment.

Credit reports and financial records are hardly the last word on how qualified an applicant is for a job. It's up to you to check other references and sources of information.

School Records

To get most "good" jobs these days, an applicant needs at least an undergraduate degree. That's why so many applicants embellish their academic credentials.

College transcripts and other school records can be valuable in helping you verify an applicant's educational background, especially if the prospective employee is in line for a key management or technical slot. Like other private documents, however, school records are shielded by federal and state laws. Also, school records sometimes contain medical information (see following section), making it doubly hard for you to gain access to them.

The Federal Family Educational and Privacy Act of 1974, commonly known as the Buckley amendment, is the primary vehicle for protecting the privacy of school records. Under this act, only students, former students, and parents of students under the age of 18 can obtain records from any educational institution receiving federal funds. Exceptions to the Buckley amendment include authorized releases, or releases decreed by a court order, subpoena, or administrative summons.

Actually, it's all right for schools to tell you when (and whether) prospective employees graduated, how long they attended, what kind of degrees they received, and what their majors and minors were. But only a former student can ask the school to send a verified copy of his or her transcript or to release sensitive information such as class rank to you. If you get hold of these records without the applicant's permission, the applicant can sue you under the Family Educational and Privacy Act, which also provides for penalties against the school that releases the records to you.

To ensure no one has a chance to fiddle with an applicant's school records, it's best for the applicant to supply them directly to you. Compliance with your request for school records should be voluntary, but you're not obligated to hire an applicant who doesn't go along with such a request.

Obtaining school records under false pretenses, as the insurance company did in the example at the beginning of the chapter, is against the law. But take heart: It's also a crime in some states (though usually no more than a misdemeanor) for prospective employees to fudge their educational background. And if you become aware of any fabricated credentials after an applicant is hired, you can use them as grounds for dismissal.

Medical Records

American employers have come a long way in their attitude toward hiring (and, where necessary, helping) employees with medical problems and disabilities. Federal and state laws have had a lot to do with this new-found interest. As I noted earlier, the Federal Rehabilitation Act of 1973 prohibits discrimination against applicants with disabilities, and Title VII of the Civil Rights Act of 1964 prevents employers from using "medical condition" as an excuse not to hire applicants. (Under Title VII, pregnancy is a medical condition.)

As you might expect, federal and state laws also protect the privacy of an employee's medical records. At the state level, physician-patient confidentiality precludes access to an individual's medical file. In other words, you cannot simply call up an applicant's doctor and ask about medical problems, psychiatric treatment, or medication unless these things legitimately affect the applicant's ability to do the job.

Likewise, you can't ask a female applicant if she is currently or intends to become pregnant. And questions about the possibility of AIDS are absolutely forbidden in many jurisdictions.

There are a few exceptions to the almost-sacrosanct rule of patient confidentiality. You can ask for medical information from applicants if:

1. The applicant's health affects his or her ability to do the job—for instance, if the work demands great physical stamina, quick reflexes, or superb hearing.
2. Your company is part of a regulated industry, such as aviation, transportation, or mining, where health and safety are prime concerns. If a pilot applying for a job with a major airline is under treatment for a drinking problem, for example, he or she must tell the potential employer about it.
3. The employee will be working in, say, a rural area in a Third World country where medical facilities may be poor.

4. The employee will be working in a country that bars foreign nationals with certain illnesses. Chinese work permit requirements now demand a negative AIDS test, for example.

You can sometimes justify the need to examine confidential medical records, especially in evaluating applicants for physically or psychologically demanding jobs. As always, though, the applicant must voluntarily give you permission to look at the records, and the information requested must have something to do with the job's qualifications.

Your company's on-site physician is allowed to examine an applicant and pass on the results to the personnel office because the physician works for the company and not for the patient. But the personnel office must still maintain the confidentiality of the exam results.

Personnel Records

Personnel records are confidential in most states, and it's against the law to disclose them without permission. This means you can't look at personnel records from an applicant's previous jobs without the applicant's consent. Even then, the applicant has the right to review the records in advance and, if he or she chooses, to authorize the release only of certain sections. And once the applicant gives you any personnel records, you must guard their privacy.

Previous employers have to be very careful about the information they give to prospective employers, too. Before sending out an applicant's records, the former employer should go over them for incorrect or possibly misleading statements. Failure to cull out such errors may mean a defamation-of-character suit, and the kinds of damages they're awarding these days in defamation cases are a stiff price to pay for carelessness.

OTHER PRIVACY ISSUES

One thing should be very clear to you by now:

The law aggressively guards individual privacy.

To bolster the safeguards I've described, there are many federal and state laws that protect an employee's right to privacy. Most of them aim at preventing the following infractions:

Discriminating against Protected Groups. Laws such as the Equal Employment Opportunity Act prohibit employers from using personal records to make employment decisions that might have an adverse effect on a racial, ethnic, religious, or political group, especially if the employer can't justify the potential adverse effect as being related to the job. Also, employers cannot ask applicants whether they are married, engaged, divorced, or living with someone unless there's a possibility of nepotism.

Under the antidiscrimination laws, a political or religious organization is allowed to dig into an applicant's personal records to hire members of the same party or faith. But other employers who try this are asking for some nasty litigation.

Showing Anti-Union Bias. Laws such as the National Labor Relations Act give job applicants the right to petition the government to reverse an employer's decision not to hire the applicant because that person is involved with a union. These laws also forbid employers from singling out applicants with union backgrounds as troublemakers or hooligans. Of course, this doesn't mean that employers have to cave in to union pressure to hire underqualified applicants.

Monitoring Applicants' Telephone Calls. Listening in on phone calls is a touchy matter at best. In some states, an employer can listen in on or tape *current employees'* calls under certain circumstances. For instance, telephone companies can monitor their operators to ensure that the operators are following phone company policy. Employers also have the right to insist that their phones be used only for business purposes, so a boss can monitor an employee's calls if he or she suspects that the employee is making too many personal calls on company time.

The thing to remember is that you cannot legally monitor a job applicant's phone calls from your company facilities. If the applicant comes on board as a permanent or temporary employee, that's another story. To be on the safe side, however, never monitor or tape a job applicant's calls.

Wiretapping.   Both the federal government and the states consider wiretapping, or any other interception of telephone communications, a criminal offense. Only law enforcement officials can perform wiretapping, and even they need a court order. In other words, don't put a tap on an applicant's phone—you could find yourself in very hot water.

Using Truth Determinants.   Many states have reined in an employer's right to use tests or other means of determining the truth of an applicant's statements. You can't force an employee to take an honesty test, be hypnotized, or undergo a psychological evaluation or handwriting analysis. If you do ask employees to take a truth test of some kind, make sure they know the purpose of the test and why you're asking them to take it.

MAKE PRIVACY WORK FOR YOU

Believe it or not, it's possible to strike a balance between your right (and need) to find out the truth about a job applicant's credentials and the applicant's right to privacy. You *can* get the information you need without trampling all over an applicant's privacy rights! Here's how to go about it:

1. Formulate a legal, companywide policy for privacy in hiring; put it in writing, and stick to it.
2. Describe your company privacy policy to the applicant, and let him or her know what role it plays in the screening process.
3. Educate your managers about sensitive ways to obtain information without violating an applicant's privacy.
4. Make sure the information you collect is directly related to the position the applicant is vying for. Don't probe into the applicant's personal life, politics, and so on unless they have something to do with the job.
5. Keep test results and other sensitive personal information confidential and secure.
6. Separate medical test results from other personnel records to ensure compliance with state medical record privacy laws.

7. Limit access to the applicant's file only to authorized personnel who really need to use the information.
8. Regulate and limit interdepartmental sharing of sensitive information about job applicants.
9. Avoid defamatory remarks, unauthorized exchanges of information, and anything else that might seem discriminatory.
10. Stay on top of legislative and regulatory changes in privacy law, especially those that might affect your preemployment practices.

And don't ever forget this cardinal rule:

If you want to look at an applicant's personal records, get his or her permission in writing.

CHAPTER 3

THE BEST PERSON
FOR THE JOB

When you recruit and screen prospective employees, you're looking for people who can do the work competently and who won't cause you trouble or make waves. But sometimes not hiring the right applicant can make more waves than hiring the wrong one:

• A small trucking company in rural western Pennsylvania places an advertisement for part-time drivers. The ad reads, "We are looking for a few good men with the stamina to drive big rigs." A qualified female driver applies for the job and is hired—but at a lower salary than the male drivers. She sues under the Federal Equal Pay Act of 1967.

• A Los Angeles exporting firm retains a "headhunter" to find a manager for its Tokyo office. The president of the firm, a staunch member of the old-boy network, hints to the headhunter that he isn't really interested in applicants who aren't male. Picking up on this cue, the headhunter eventually finds a male candidate who has most of the qualifications for the job. A female applicant with far more outstanding qualifications doesn't even get an interview for the position. She files a complaint under California's antidiscrimination laws against both the headhunter and the exporting firm.

• A New Jersey grocery chain, afraid that it will inadvertently hire people with AIDS, decides to make a practice of finding out all it can about each applicant's history of recent hospitalization; the management thinks this approach will zero in on people with AIDS because they spend so much time in the hospital. But one canny applicant becomes suspicious about the questions.

Because he figures his rights are being violated, he files a complaint with the state human rights commission.

Identifying the skills and attributes required to do a job is easy—you know what you want and need. Finding an applicant who has those skills and attributes is a lot tougher. If you're like many employers these days, you're going to get at least get 25 résumés for every opening. Somehow, you must cull out the wheat from the chaff. To get the right person for the job, you need to recruit a pool of well-qualified applicants and carefully select the ones you think deserve further consideration. That's just common-sense personnel practice.

Unfortunately, screening is the sand trap of the employment game. Play it wrong, and you're sure to end up with an antidiscrimination suit. No court or law has ever said that you can't screen prospective employees to find the best one for the job—you just can't violate anyone's civil rights in the process.

LAWS TO WATCH OUT FOR

Although Title VII of the Civil Rights Act and the Age Discrimination in Employment Act catch most of the headlines in hiring-related litigation today, several other important federal laws and regulations can trip you up when you're recruiting and selecting job applicants.

Federal Equal Pay Act

"Equal pay for equal work" used to be nothing more than a rallying cry at feminist gatherings. Since the late 1960s, however, the concept has become firmly entrenched in federal law

The Federal Equal Pay Act of 1967 makes it illegal for an employer to hire an employee of one sex at a different rate of pay than the other sex receives for the same work. If the job requires the same skills, effort, and responsibilities, you cannot pay a female applicant a lower salary than a male applicant. And you certainly can't pay a male applicant more than a female applicant if both are going to be working in the same place and under the same conditions.

The wage-hour administrator at the U.S. Department of Labor oversees the Equal Pay Act, which applies to all employers and employees covered by the minimum wage and overtime provisions of the Federal Fair Labor Standards Act. Some recent amendments to the Equal Pay Act have extended its coverage to employees who may be exempt from overtime pay requirements, such as technical professionals, executives, and managers.

Equal Protection Clause

The 13th and 14th amendments to the U.S. Constitution were enacted to bring an end to slavery in the United States, but the courts have given these amendments a much wider charter over the years. For instance, many courts have stated that the 14th Amendment prohibits public agencies and private employers alike from discriminating against job applicants because of their race, color, or religion. But applicants are increasingly using the Equal Protection Clause to sue public agencies and are relying on other legal vehicles to sue private employers for discrimination in hiring.

Civil Rights Act of 1866

Even though the 13th and 14th amendments quickly became part of the Constitution during the Civil War, the events of the Reconstruction made it clear that the newly freed slaves weren't getting enough of a fair shake under the law. In 1866, Congress enacted the first of several federal acts to ban discrimination in employment and other spheres of American life on the basis of an individual's race or religion.

The Civil Rights Act of 1866 originally was intended to apply only to discrimination in hiring by the government, but the courts have extended it to cover private employers, too. In fact, job applicants have already used the act as grounds for suing employers who discriminate on the basis of race in their screening and selection practices. Some courts have even extended the act to cover discrimination because of an applicant's status as a legal alien or because the applicant's family lives outside the United States.

The courts haven't gone so far as to extend the 1866 act to sex discrimination in hiring by private employers. Nevertheless, they have applied it to cases of sex discrimination in hiring by the government.

As far as an applicant is concerned, there are several advantages to using the 1866 act in a suit against a potential employer. For one thing, the applicant doesn't have to go through the Equal Employment Opportunity Commission (EEOC) first, as Title VII of the Civil Rights Act of 1964 demands; he or she can take the case directly to court. For another, the applicant can use the 1866 act as a vehicle for filing a suit independent of Title VII. Finally, the 1866 act lets the applicant sue an employer who hasn't been named in an EEOC action.

Civil Rights Act of 1871

Bolstering the Equal Protection Clause and the 1866 act, section 1983 of the Civil Rights Act of 1871 allows an applicant to sue an employer who acts on the direct or indirect instructions of a government official to deprive the applicant of such federally guaranteed rights as equality in employment. And section 1985(3) of the act makes it illegal for employers to form a "conspiracy" to deny applicants access to employment opportunities because of their race.

What this means is that the mayor can't drop hints to the shopkeepers on Main Street not to hire blacks or other members of minority groups, nor can the mayor collude with the town council to pass a local ordinance that prevents employers from hiring blacks or sets quotas for the number of minority-group applicants who can be hired.

Job applicants have successfully wielded the 1871 act against police departments, transportation authorities, boards of education, semipublic hospitals, and even state employment agencies. The courts have also stated that the act justifies affirmative action or preferential hiring on the basis of race. In some cases, they've even used the act to make a prospective employer pay an applicant's legal fees.

Executive Order 11141

Under this order, federal contractors and subcontractors cannot discriminate in hiring on the basis of age. The only exceptions to the order are jobs in which age is a genuine occupational qualification, or if there's some kind of statutory requirement to hire applicants who fall within a certain age range.

WHO ARE YOUR APPLICANTS?

With so many federal and state antidiscrimination laws breathing down your neck, you're probably wondering if it's still possible to screen applicants without getting sued. No one will deny that the antidiscrimination laws have made recruiting and screening job applicants a legal minefield. Worse, the applicability of these laws varies from case to case, often depending on the type of employment involved and the status of the applicant (full-time, temporary, etc.). To play it absolutely safe, I'd recommend that you don't discriminate in recruiting or screening *any* prospective employees.

Employees of Contract Services

More and more employers are asking "employment brokers" to supply secretaries, computer operators, security guards, and other temporary employees to fill in-house jobs as needed. These workers are hired, paid, and fired by the contract employment agency.

Even though you're not directly responsible for hiring and firing "temps, " you should still be careful. *Don't* subtly convey to the contract agency that certain classes of workers aren't welcome at your company. If an employer tries to use a contract agency as a front for his or her employment prejudices, both the employer and the agency can wind up on the wrong end of an antidiscrimination suit.

Temporary Employees

Most employees are still "permanent" workers who join a company for the long haul. Some jobs, however, last only for a specified period. You may prefer to fill such vacancies with a "permanent temporary" who actually works for your company rather than for an outside employment contractor.

Even though the workers who fill these temporary slots have become a fact of life for many American companies, the legal system has not yet decided how to treat them. So far, however, I'd say that it's a good idea to apply the antidiscrimination laws to recruiting and selecting temporary employees unless you hear otherwise from the courts.

Contract Employees

Whether a contract employee is a freelance programmer who agrees to write one piece of software or an oil company executive who signs a contract to work in Saudi Arabia for several years, contract employees have a different status than full- or part-time at-will employees. That's because the contract spells out the duration and conditions of their employment.

Many of the antidiscrimination laws apply to contract employees as well as at-will employees. Therefore, you might be facing a lawsuit if, in recruiting and screening applicants for a contract position, you select applicants because of their race, religion, ethnic background, or sex instead of their ability to do the job.

Partners

Traditionally, accounting and law firms have had a lot of leeway in recruiting and selecting candidates for partnerships because the courts were reluctant to become involved in saying who could or couldn't be a partner. But that's changing fast: The courts are now standing firm on Title VII and other antidiscrimination legislation. Therefore, if you're looking for a new partner, make sure you avoid discrimination or bias in your recruitment and screening practices.

Consultants and Subcontractors

If you're a federal contractor and you want to hire a consultant, the rules are simple: Don't discriminate if you want to keep that government contract!

Executive Order 11246, which applies to federal contractors with more than $10,000 in contracts, prohibits discrimination in hiring on the basis of race, religion, sex, or national origin. Federal contractors with more than $50,000 in contracts and over 50 employees must also implement affirmative-action programs. And, as we've seen in this chapter, Executive Order 11141 makes it illegal for any federal contractor to discriminate in hiring because of age.

But nothing's quite as cut-and-dried in the private sector. Consultants are not employees in the conventional sense, as temporaries and contract workers are, so the federal antidiscrimination laws don't apply to them.

The situation is identical for subcontractors. Employers with federal contracts cannot refuse to hire a subcontractor because of race, color, religion, or national origin, but private employers aren't bound by the federal antidiscrimination laws.

Volunteers

Although volunteers aren't directly covered by federal or state preemployment and employment laws, you're asking for trouble if you discriminate in recruiting and selecting them. The various civil rights acts and common-law principles of fairness and equality protect volunteers' rights in recruitment and "hiring."

RECRUITING RIGHT

There are a lot of ways to find job applicants, ranging from simple word-of-mouth to classified ads, employment agencies, and college recruiting services. The key is to get the word out about your job opportunity and the kinds of applicants you want to fill it without stepping on any antidiscrimination toes.

Word-of-Mouth

A great many employees in the United States have gotten their jobs because someone mentioned something at a cocktail party or because a friend who worked for another company heard about a new position through the office grapevine. This has been going on for hundreds of years, and it will doubtless go on for hundreds more. In fact, some say that the best jobs are never advertised.

But word-of-mouth referral really depends on who's spreading the word to whom. If young, white, male workers are passing on word-of-mouth information to their young, white, male friends, you may or may not have a case of discrimination on your hands. Appearances certainly indicate, however, that other segments of the work force aren't hearing about the "best" jobs.

To get around this, many states have enacted laws that prohibit subtle efforts to misuse word-of-mouth to restrict hiring on the basis of age, sex, race, religion, or national origin. Under these laws, an employer could get in trouble by asking employees to tell only white male applicants about a high-level management job.

Advertising

Under Title VII of the Civil Rights Act of 1964, an employer cannot print or publish job advertisements or notices that indicate a preference for applicants of a specific race, sex, religion, ethnic background, and so forth. Sly efforts to get around Title VII by advertising in racially or sexually segregated listings would violate Title VII, as would an advertisement for "Help Wanted—Male." But placing an ad in a widely read publication such as *Ebony* or *Glamour* can effectively counter charges of discrimination against blacks or women.

If you don't want to risk running afoul of Title VII, make sure your advertisement or notice uses only neutral, nonsexist job titles such as "salesperson" or "manager." If the ad contains a non-neutral job title, it should also include the designation "male/female" to show that you welcome applicants of both sexes.

If you're a federal contractor or subcontractor, your recruitment efforts must comply with Executive Order 11246 as well as Title VII. Therefore, your job advertisements must:

1. State that all qualified applicants will receive consideration without regard to race, color, religion, sex, or national origin.
2. Use a display ad that includes an appropriate insignia from the Office of Federal Contract Compliance.
3. Always use the phrase "An equal-opportunity employer." (If your ad runs with others in a group, you must make

sure that all the companies in that group are also equal-opportunity employers.)

Electronic Bulletin Boards

The number of individuals and businesses linked by networks and on-line information services with access to electronic "bulletin boards" has skyrocketed. Not surprisingly, more and more companies are turning to these bulletin boards to advertise job postings, especially in the high-tech sector.

You should know before you post that federal and state anti-discrimination laws apply to electronic as well as print job advertisements. Moreover, the bulletin boards fall under the aegis of the Federal Communications Commission, which prohibits the use of communication systems to promote discriminatory employment practices.

Recruiting Agencies

Employment and other agencies that actively recruit job applicants must follow Title VII antidiscrimination guidelines and the Age Discrimination in Employment Act. In fact, recruiting agencies should be particularly sensitive to age discrimination guidelines because many companies will try to pressure them into finding young applicants.

The Age Discrimination in Employment Act clearly specifies that recruitment on the basis of age is against the law unless age is a bona fide occupational qualification. Company or campus recruiters and employment agency staffers should thus be careful not to use terms such as *young, boy,* or *retired* in describing the qualifications for a position. And recruiters should never say that the ideal candidate should be "between 25 to 38" or, much worse, that no one "between 40 and 50" need apply. But the recruiter can ask whether the applicant is less than 40 years old, whether he or she has a work permit, and when he or she attended college.

Recruiting agencies are autonomous entities. Nonetheless, an employer who knows (or has reason to suspect) that an agency discriminates in hiring, and continues to use that agency, may be just as liable under the hiring laws as the agency itself. Likewise, employers shouldn't deal with recruiting agencies that use discriminatory tests in screening job applicants.

Campus Recruiting

The EEOC and local human rights commissions take a dim view of employers who limit their recruiting *only* to a same-sex or same-race college. You can avoid the appearance of discrimination in campus recruiting, however, if you give both sides equal time and send recruiters to, say, all-male *and* all-female colleges. Using women and members of minority groups as campus recruiters can also deflect charges of discrimination.

Affirmative Action

Occasionally, the EEOC or a court order compels an employer to give preference to members of minority groups or women in recruitment and hiring. This sort of thing usually comes about because the EEOC wants to balance the inequities resulting from past discrimination. But sometimes EEOC prodding isn't necessary: A company can voluntarily set its own goals and timetables to recruit more members of minority groups for its work force.

The courts have had no difficulty upholding affirmative-action programs established under Executive Order 11246 by federal contractors and subcontractors. In the private sector, however, some applicants and employers have begun to challenge affirmative action by claiming "reverse discrimination" under, interestingly, the Civil Rights Act of 1964.

Avoid Recruiting Hassles

It really isn't that hard to steer clear of the dreaded "appearance of bias" in your recruitment campaigns and applicant selection procedures, as long as you follow these simple guidelines:

1. Consider developing a special recruitment program for minority-group members and women.
2. If you work with a recruiting agency or headhunter, be sure to choose one that makes reasonable efforts to seek out qualified minority and female applicants.
3. If you advertise a position, make sure that the newspaper or magazine carrying the ad reaches members of minority groups and others protected by Title VII.

4. As an alternative, directly advertise the position in publications aimed at minority groups or female readers.
5. Advertise for qualified job candidates on radio or TV—the broadcast media reach just about everybody!
6. Participate in job fairs, conferences, and other recruitment efforts sponsored by minority groups, women, and so on.
7. Tap groups such as the Urban League, the National Organization for Women, and the National Association for the Advancement of Colored People for qualified job applicants.
8. Send recruiters to speak to local minority-group organizations about job opportunities at your company.
9. Actively recruit from professional schools with large concentrations of minority groups and female students.
10. Encourage members of minority groups and women at your company to refer qualified neighbors, friends, and (if you don't have a nepotism rule) relatives for positions with your organization.
11. Invite minority-group and female applicants to contact your personnel department directly.
12. Make sure that your company's job-solicitation brochures indicate that there's a place for minorities and women in your organization.

THE JOB APPLICATION

After you spread the word about a position, get ready to wade through the flood of résumés and applications you'll probably receive in response to your ad or recruitment campaign!

Even if applicants supply a résumé, it's a good idea to have them fill out your company's job application form, too. The application form should give you enough preliminary information to start culling out the hotshots from the less promising candidates. (How to read between the lines of a résumé will be covered in Chapter 4.)

Whether you're creating an application form for the first time or revising an existing form to cover more bases, you need to think carefully about the kind of information you want to elicit from prospective employees. You'll probably want to design your application to answer some or all of these general questions that apply to many jobs:

1. Of what country is the applicant a citizen? (This information is often required by law.)
2. Where does the applicant live? How long has he or she lived in the state?
3. Has the applicant been employed under different names or aliases?
4. What foreign languages does the applicant speak, read, or write? (This is especially important if your company has overseas branches or if certain jobs demand fluency in a language other than English.)
5. What is the applicant's highest level of education?
6. What kind of work experience has the applicant had? What are the names and addresses of his or her previous employers?
7. Has the applicant served in the military?
8. What are the names of the applicant's parents?
9. What are the names of the applicant's spouse and children?
10. Who should the company notify if the applicant has an accident or some other on-the-job emergency?
11. Who are the applicant's character references?

By having the prospective employee answer these questions right on the application, you can save yourself a lot of grief later on.

The application and screening period is also a good time to take care of preliminaries that will allow you to do more in-depth background checks and to lay the groundwork for a fair and aboveboard employer-employee relationship:

1. Ask the applicant to provide you with all legally obtainable records relevant to the job—college transcripts, personnel records, and so forth.
2. Let the applicant know that the information he or she furnishes must be accurate, at least to his or her ability to re-

member. In other words, inform the applicant that altering transcripts or other records will be reason enough not to hire him or her.

3. Tell the applicant that any significant omissions in his or her educational or employment history will be grounds for refusal to hire.

4. Require the applicant to agree to comply with your organization's policies as a condition of employment.

5. If the law *demands* that prospective employees undergo testing before being hired for a particular job, or *allows* employers to conduct preemployment testing for any job, explain this to the applicant, and ask him or her to submit to the tests. Under certain conditions, you can compel an applicant to submit to drug testing as a condition of employment.

6. Let the applicant know that employers can, with a few exceptions, legally monitor their employees' telephone calls and video display terminals, and ask the applicant to submit to this kind of technological "snooping" as a condition of employment.

7. If an applicant has worked in jobs in which he or she handled cash or checks, be sure to find out why he or she left those jobs.

8. As a condition of employment, require the applicant to follow the work schedule that you set out, as long as it conforms to federal and state employment laws.

When you're reviewing and processing job applications, be careful! You might not be aware, for instance, that the applicant is responsible *only* for information supplied on the date that he or she fills out the application form. In general, don't process an application more than three months old unless the applicant has a chance to go over it and make any necessary changes first.

Also, ensure that you personally witness the applicant's signature on his or her application form, or make arrangements to have the signature witnessed by someone trustworthy or notarized. If you take this small precaution, it's easy to avoid one of those messy situations where the applicant claims that he or she didn't sign the application form or provide the information on it.

WHAT THE LAW LETS YOU DO

The U.S. workplace has rightly been called the most regulated in the world. Nonetheless, employers *can* impose certain minimum standards on applicants, as long as they don't violate employment law. You have the legal right to:

1. Impose height and weight requirements if they're necessary to ensure safety and efficiency on the job.
2. Enforce physical fitness qualifications if required to carry out a particular job.
3. Refuse to hire poor credit risks if the job requires handling money and other valuables.
4. Refuse to hire an applicant who isn't willing to accept the work hours you request of all employees.
5. Refuse to hire any person who fails to produce evidence that he or she has a valid work permit. (This is a requirement of the new U.S. immigration laws, which will be covered in more detail later.)
6. Refuse to hire an applicant who does not go along with your reasonable efforts to accommodate his or her religious practices.
7. Refuse to hire an applicant who is not a U.S. citizen (for instance, if you are a federal contractor working on a top-secret government project).
8. Refuse to spend a lot of money to hire an applicant, unless these expenses are mandated by law.
9. Refuse to hire an employee who does not go along with a companywide ban on smoking that was enacted for health and safety.
10. Require a prospective employee to work on Saturdays and Sundays, as long as you're not trying to single out members of certain religious denominations.
11. Require a prospective employee to be "bondable," providing that the job in question actually demands fidelity bonding.
12. Require all applicants to conform to the company's seniority system or employee benefit plan.
13. Carry out a job-related preemployment investigation of the applicant.

14. Ask a female applicant her maiden name, especially if you need this information to conduct a preemployment investigation.
15. Ask questions about the applicant's past salaries and benefits.
16. Consider performance reports from previous employers in evaluating an applicant, unless they're discriminatory.

The preemployment laws aren't there to prevent you from hiring the people you want to hire or to force you into hiring the people you don't. Admittedly, it's tough to stay on top of all the federal and state antidiscrimination laws. But you don't have to spend hours in law libraries in order to recruit and screen right, as long as you stick to this guideline:

**Avoid the appearance of bias in recruitment
and screening.**

If you follow the advice given in this chapter, you shouldn't have any trouble finding the best possible person for the job!

CHAPTER 4

BACKGROUND AND REFERENCE CHECKS

Nearly 30 percent of all job applicants lie on their résumés and during employment interviews, according to a study conducted by Equifax Services, Inc., of Atlanta. These lies run the gamut from making up academic degrees and job titles to providing phony references. It gets worse, too: *Security* magazine noted that in a review of 11,000 job applications, 448 applicants had neglected to mention convictions for drug use, rape, and other serious crimes.

Well, what if some employees lie about the skeletons in their closets? Can't you just fire them when you find out and be done with it? Unfortunately, it's not that simple:

• An applicant for a high-level position with a New York security firm had an impressive résumé and seemed to be the best person for the job in every possible way. Still, the firm figured it should check some of his references before hiring him, so the personnel manager talked to the applicant's best friend, next-door neighbor, and former boss. They had nothing but good things to say about the applicant, and he got the job. Soon after being hired, however, he stole thousands of dollars from one of the firm's clients.

In the ensuing lawsuit, the personnel manager argued that he had carried out all the necessary checks and hadn't run across anything questionable in the applicant's background. But the judge didn't buy it: Employers, she noted, have an obligation to dig as deep as they can without violating an applicant's privacy rights.

• The manager of an apartment complex raped a tenant. It turned out that he had spent eight years in jail for a similar crime. The apartment complex owners had questioned the eight-year gap in his résumé when he applied for the job, but they trustingly believed him when he said he'd spent that time working overseas. Naïveté is no excuse under the law, however. The apartment complex owners wound up paying hefty damages to their former tenant.

• In Washington, D.C., agents of the Immigration and Naturalization Service (INS) raided a restaurant and arrested several employees for working in violation of the Immigration Reform Control Act. Their employer hadn't checked their "green cards" or done anything else to confirm that they were legal workers; again, he'd just taken their word for it. The employer's slipup cost him plenty in fines and other penalties.

As these examples show, failure to do a careful check of an applicant's work history and references can mean stiff civil penalties for an employer if the applicant harms an innocent person after being hired. But employers also have a personal stake in doing background checks—the billions of dollars that dishonest employees steal from their companies every year.

Background and reference checks are playing an increasingly pivotal role in the hiring process today. Of course, probing beneath an applicant's shining surface isn't always easy or even possible when you have all those sticky privacy issues to contend with. Nonetheless, a thorough and effective program for doing background and reference checks is imperative if you want to protect yourself and your company.

UNLOCKING A RÉSUMÉ'S SECRETS

Opinion Research Corp. recently subjected a number of résumés to a "truth check." The results were disturbing: As many as 80 percent of the résumés surveyed gave misleading information about the applicant's employment history while another 30 percent listed false academic credentials.

Not all job applicants lie on their résumés, of course, but quite a few bend the truth if they think it will help them get a job in today's dog-eat-dog labor market. Professional résumé services can make the waters even muddier if they know what they're doing. But there are ways to tell if a résumé is straight out of *Grimm's Fairy Tales*—you just have to know what to look for.

Work History

Faking or concealing employment history information is probably the most pervasive type of résumé fraud. All too many applicants lengthen the time spent at a job, give the names of nonexistent or "ghost" employers, or boost salary levels.

But this is small-potatoes fakery when you consider how many applicants try to hide prison sentences, psychiatric illnesses, and other truly damaging information from prospective employers. Take the managerial candidate who "forgot" to tell a Boston bank that the U.S. Securities and Exchange Commission had sued him for insider trading, or the airline ticket agent who claimed to have worked for another airline for five years but who had actually spent two of those years in a drug rehabilitation program.

You can prevent embarrassing incidents such as these by digging as deep as you legally can into an applicant's work history. That might mean checking with listed references, former employers, workers at the applicant's previous job, licensing boards, and more. You can do the digging yourself or contract with an outside agency to do it for you.

Job Titles and Responsibilities

Job title inflation is another widespread résumé fraud. Applicants often try to give themselves a little extra status by exaggerating or making up job titles. An applicant might claim to have been a "sales manager, " for instance, when he or she was really just another member of the sales force who occasionally did a few managerial tasks when the boss was out of town.

This kind of puffery tends to go hand-in-hand with spurious tales about the applicant's on-the-job achievements. An applicant might say that he or she managed a branch office, supervised an entire sales force, created a new department, or was instrumental in developing a company's sizzling marketing strategy. What such applicants leave out are such "trivial" matters as the size of the office, the budget that the department handled, or the number of employees the applicant actually supervised.

Compensation

Salary and benefit padding is common, especially when an applicant is seeking a higher-level position than he or she held in the past. For instance, an applicant may bundle every possible benefit, including year-end bonuses, into his or her salary to inflate the total figure. But it shouldn't be too hard for you to check out an applicant's previous salary; most employers will release salary information if authorized by a current or previous employee.

Self-Employment

Applicants who've been in prison or unemployed for a long period often state on their résumés that they spent this time working as freelancers or "independent consultants." They frequently get away with this because self-employment is one of the toughest résumé claims for employers to verify. After all, plenty of people are legitimately in business for themselves; the entrepreneurial spirit is what our free-market economy is all about.

Actually, though, it *is* possible to confirm claims of self-employment if you're willing to put in a little extra effort. Among the things you should check out are the applicant's previous addresses (don't be surprised if one of them turns out to be the state penitentiary!), professional and business associates, former clients, bank references, credit history, and (if the applicant has incorporated his or her business) corporate records. You can also examine court or county clerk records, talk to licensing boards or professional organizations to which the applicant may have belonged, or check with a local regulatory agency.

Education and Training

Fabricated employment histories and puffed-up job titles or salaries are number one on the list of résumé scams in survey after survey, but faked educational credentials and professional training run a close second.

Competition for high-paying technical and professional jobs has become so fierce that applicants will make up prestigious academic credentials to get a foot in the door. For example, an engineer with a large electronics firm claimed to have graduate degrees in physics and mathematics, and to have done high-level research at five universities. A belated background check showed that he had never even received an undergraduate degree.

In a similar case, a Chicago anesthesiologist stated on his résumé that he held degrees from Yale and Columbia and had done his anesthesiology residency at the Walter Reed Army Hospital in Washington, D.C. Apparently, no one at the hospital that hired him thought to question this impressive educational roster. The anesthesiologist participated in more than 70 surgical procedures without a hitch. Then one of his patients had a heart attack while undergoing an operation. The resulting inquiry revealed that the anesthesiologist was a quack: He'd fabricated all his academic credentials and professional medical experience.

Résumé frauds involving education come in all shapes and sizes. Applicants who may have attended college for only a year or two tell prospective employers that they hold a bachelor's degree. A few have even assumed the identity of a real graduate!

Some applicants say that they attended a well-known business school to work on an MBA; what they leave out is that they never actually received the degree. Others lie about PhD degrees—a fairly easy thing to get away with, considering the many steps involved in getting one. An applicant might tell a prospective employer that he or she has, say, all the credits for a PhD and just needs to finish up the orals or thesis.

Then there are the applicants who buy mail-order degrees from unaccredited universities in the United States or abroad. Academic fraud becomes especially difficult to detect when foreign universities are involved. If a country has been ravaged by war or civil strife, records may have been destroyed, making it conveniently difficult to verify an applicant's credentials. But international professional groups and the U.S. Department of Education in Washington, D.C., can give you some help if you need it.

Honors and Awards

If you put together all the bogus awards, honors, and publications listed on résumés, there'd probably be one for every job applicant in the country! The American Society for Industrial Security says that an overwhelming number of job applicants puff up their professional achievements.

You'll want to make sure an applicant's accomplishments are real, so ask him or her for copies of the published articles or proof of the award or honor received—a copy of the certificate or a photograph of the trophy.

You can easily check out bogus memberships in professional organizations by contacting those groups. Likewise, if you suspect that an organization itself might be phony despite its impressive name, it's not hard to find out if the organization exists and has a good reputation.

Recommendations

Letters of recommendation from former employers are not always a reliable yardstick of an applicant's on-the-job performance. Some employers are afraid to put the true story down in writing; others may just want to pass on a problem worker to someone else.

By reading between the lines you can usually tell if a former employer's recommendation is worth the paper it's written on. A brief, general letter that might apply to any worker should be a red flag to you. Employers who don't want to give honest recommendations try to avoid specifics or subjective comments which can come back to haunt them if the truth ever surfaces.

Résumé Red-Alerts

As we have seen, résumé fakers can be very clever and devious, making credentials fraud particularly hard to catch. But they often tip their hand by:

1. Giving "out-of-business" employers. If a company listed on a résumé really isn't in business any longer, check to see how long it was in business and whether the dates on the applicant's résumé match the company's life span.

2. Omitting a period of employment or stretching employment dates.
3. Listing a long period of joblessness or a long string of low-paying jobs, especially if the applicant is a college graduate. Sometimes these things are subterfuges for a prison term.
4. Making misleading or exaggerated claims of expertise or experience.
5. Listing colleges or universities with names similar to famous institutions of higher education, such as Yale College of El Paso, Texas. Be particularly careful here: A lot of these similar-sounding colleges are just degree mills that capitalize on name recognition.
6. Assuming the identity of an established professional in a field. Believe it or not, some résumé fakers are brazen enough to try this, so ask for proof of identification during the preemployment period. One con artist pretended to be a well-respected manager, but the company that hired him found out inadvertently (and luckily) that he was not who he claimed to be.
7. "Forgetting" to list some past employers. In one case I know of, an applicant "forgot" to mention that he had worked as a hotel clerk for three months. A check revealed that he had been fired for allegedly stealing petty cash from the hotel.
8. Giving the names and telephone numbers of friends as supervisory references. Many of these phony supervisors work at the same company the applicant formerly worked at, so you might not catch the scam unless you check with others (especially legitimate supervisors) at the company.
9. Providing you directly with a college transcript instead of asking the college to send a verified copy to your office. Applicants have been known to doctor their college transcripts.
10. Listing supplementary education, such as conferences, training programs, courses, and so on. Some applicants send friends to conferences and training programs in their place, so be sure to verify that the applicant ac-

tually attended the postgraduate program or extension courses on his or her résumé. You might also want to find out if the applicant took the supplementary training merely to puff up his or her educational credentials: A couple of courses at the Harvard extension school do not a Harvard BA make.

11. Describing job shifts that do not reflect advancement within an organization. Be on guard also for fuzzy descriptions of the applicant's duties and responsibilities at previous jobs.

12. Using unacceptable grammar, spelling, and punctuation; allowing typos and illegibility, and using a nonstandard layout. The résumé's mechanics can say a lot about the applicant's level of training, professionalism, and educational background.

13. Describing career goals that are unrealistic or irrelevant to the job the applicant is seeking. Be suspicious of pie-in-the-sky goals.

Keep in mind that résumé fraud is not limited to any one industry or region of the United States. American workers like to move around, so résumé scams are widespread in every business. Résumé fraud isn't endemic to any particular part of the work force, either. Job applicants at every rung of the corporate ladder, from entry-level workers to CEOs, tell "little white lies" on their résumés. So, while it may sound a bit paranoid, you really can't take a résumé at face value any more.

EN GARDE AGAINST RÉSUMÉ FRAUD

If you hire an applicant with falsified credentials, you're likely to get someone who does a shoddy job—and that's the *good* news. Hire someone with a hidden criminal record, and you run the risk of that employee stealing your property or assets, or even violently attacking co-workers. But you don't have to let unscrupulous applicants get away with résumé fakery if you follow this advice:

1. Never hesitate to verify the applicant's credentials. Start with telephone calls to former employers, references, schools, and so on, and follow up your calls with letters.

2. Ask the applicant to provide W-2 forms, a social security card, a birth certificate, and other forms of identification to confirm his or her identity and past employment. Obtaining these credentials is especially important when hiring low-level employees. (Later in this chapter, I'll detail the kind of employee identification demanded by recent immigration laws.)

3. Ask the applicant to sign a statement regarding the veracity of his or her credentials and other materials. You can incorporate this statement into the job application or simply give it to the applicant to sign separately. Whatever format you choose, make sure the statement is witnessed or notarized.

4. Let the applicant know right from the start that it is company policy to fire any employee who has fabricated his or her credentials. This warning should deflate any "wrongful discharge" suits the employee may try to file if he or she is fired for fudging background information.

Thoroughly checking out everything that needs to be checked on a résumé may seem daunting, particularly if you must sift through hundreds of applications and résumés every month. Of course, you're not going to subject every applicant to this kind of scrutiny. If a candidate seems promising, though, leave no stone unturned.

I've already talked about the hot water employers can get into if they violate applicants' privacy rights by obtaining personal information without permission. Figure 4–1 shows an all-purpose release form; if an applicant signs it, he or she is giving you permission to obtain just about any information you need to conduct a comprehensive background check. You should explain what the form means and why you need this information before giving it to him or her to sign. And definitely make sure the applicant's signature is notarized or witnessed.

Public Information Sources

There are many fruitful secondary sources you can tap to evaluate whether an applicant is telling the truth on his or her résumé. In fact, some private verification firms that check credentials say

FIGURE 4–1
Sample Record Release Form

The undersigned [name of job applicant], in connection with this application, authorizes all corporations, companies, credit agencies, educational institutions, persons, law enforcement agencies, military services, and former employers to release information they may have about me to [name of employer] or its agents, and to release them from any liability or responsibility for doing so. In addition, I authorize the procurement of an investigative consumer report and understand that such a report may contain information about my background, character, and personal reputation. This notice will also apply to any future update reports that may be requested.

Signature [name of applicant]

Witness [name of witness]

Date of signing

that more than 300 public sources are readily available to the employer who wants to use them for evaluating an applicant's credentials.

One nice thing about these sources is that most of them are open to the public, so you don't necessarily have to get an applicant's permission to look at them. Best of all, however, such checks are perfectly legal.

If you don't want to spend hours at the courthouse poring through bins of microfilm or heaps of dusty records, you can use in-house agencies, such as your company's security department, or hire an outside investigator to do the digging for you. Most likely, however, you (or the person you delegate the investigation to) will be able to get the information you need with a few phone calls.

Corporate Records. If an applicant claims to have owned his or her own business or to have worked for a now-defunct corporation, you can check with the secretary of state for the area in which the company was incorporated or based to confirm whether it ever existed and, if so, how long it was around. A phone call to the secretary's office can often get you the names of the original incorporators, directors, and registered agent, and the address of the firm.

Limited Partnerships. It's possible to glean information on partnerships from local tax offices, licensing boards (if professionals are involved), and state and local better business bureaus and chambers of commerce. The records are public and should provide you with helpful information.

Court Records. Litigation records, whether civil or criminal, are public documents. Many are also on computer, which means that a phone call to the courts in the applicant's jurisdiction can easily confirm whether he or she has been the target of a lawsuit or criminal prosecution. Once you've identified such a case, it's easy to obtain copies of the file by mail. To save time, you can simply send a member of your security staff or an outside investigator down to the courthouse to take a look at the record and get a copy for you.

Arrest Records. Although *conviction* records are public and can be obtained from any city, county, state, or federal court in which the prosecution was conducted, *arrest* records are not always public. Whether they are depends on state law and on the crime for which the applicant may have been arrested. Juvenile arrest records are always confidential, and FBI arrest records are closed to the public by federal law.

Vehicle Records. If a job involves a lot of driving (particularly in a company car), you might want to obtain an applicant's vehicle records and a write-up of his or her driving history from the state motor vehicle bureau. State motor vehicle departments are also the prime source for checking if an applicant has been arrested for driving while intoxicated (DWI).

City and County Filings. Licenses and other commercial transactions are usually recorded in city or county courts. Examples include records of the property an applicant owns or a notice of a lien on his or her house. Again, it's easy to check out these public records.

Tax Rolls and Real Property Records. If you want to confirm an applicant's financial situation, try county tax rolls or real estate records. They're especially helpful in checking out candidates for senior executive positions.

Other public records you may want to check include voter registrations, marriage licenses, previous addresses, and professional licenses an applicant may have held.

IMMIGRATION PITFALLS

When an employer checks out credentials nowadays, one of the most important is bound to be proof of American citizenship or a "green card" allowing an alien to work in the United States. Immigration rules are getting tighter all the time; the days of letting hordes of "huddled masses" into the country are gone, probably forever. What's different about work regulations for newcomers nowadays is that employers face serious penalties for hiring illegal aliens.

It wasn't always this way. Until November 6, 1986, when President Ronald Reagan signed the Immigration Reform and Control Act (IRCA) into law, employers could hire illegal aliens with impunity—and they often did.

Under IRCA's predecessor, the Immigration and Naturalization Act of 1952, it was a case of "blame the victim": Sanctions rained on the employee. An illegal alien who worked in the United States without a permit could be deported, but the employer who hired the illegal alien escaped without a scratch. Even if an employer *knew* that the applicant would be working in violation of federal law, and went ahead and hired that applicant, the employer wouldn't even get a wrist-slap.

But that all changed with the enactment of IRCA: Employers no longer enjoy immunity from federal prosecution if they fail to do adequate checks on employees who might be illegal aliens. As of May 4, 1988, agents from the INS and the U.S. Department of Labor can refer employers who hire illegal aliens to the U.S. Department of Justice, which has both civil and criminal authority over any resulting prosecutions.

Scope of the Law

Under IRCA, you can hire only American citizens and aliens who are authorized to work in the United States. The law also requires you to verify the employment eligibility of every employee hired after November 6, 1987. To make this task easier, the INS has developed Form I-9, which employers must complete and retain to verify employment eligibility for all their employees.

No matter who an applicant is or where he or she may come from, the law demands that every employer in the United States:

1. Thoroughly check documents establishing the employee's identity and eligibility to work.
2. Instruct all employees to fill out their portion of Form I-9 when they begin work.
3. Complete the remaining portion of Form I-9.
4. Retain the form for at least three years, or for one year after a worker leaves the job, whichever comes later.
5. Present Form I-9 for inspection to all INS or Department of Labor officials on request after three days' advance notice.

Anyone hired after May 31, 1987, must complete Form I-9 within three business days of the date of hiring. If the person is hired for less than three days, the employer must complete the form before the end of the employee's first working day.

You don't need to complete the form, however, for the following workers:

- Employees hired before November 7, 1986.
- Individuals employed on an intermittent or sporadic basis.
- Laborers or others who actually work for a third-party contract employment service, such as a day-labor or temporary agency.
- Independent contractors.

Form I-9 Requirements

As I just mentioned, Form I-9 has two sections. The employee completes the first section, the employer the second.

In completing his or her section of the form, the employee must provide a document or documents that establish his or her identity and eligibility for employment. These documents fall into three groups: List A, List B, and List C. List A documents establish both identity and employment eligibility; List B documents establish identity alone, and List C establishes eligibility alone. If the prospective employee cannot provide a document from List A, he or she must produce one from List B and one from List C.

List A documents include the following:

1. U.S. passport.
2. Certificate of U.S. citizenship (INS Form N-560 or N-561).
3. Certificate of naturalization (INS Form N-550 or N-570).
4. Unexpired foreign passport.
5. Alien registration receipt card (INS Form I-151) or resident alien card (INS Form I-551), as long as it contains a photograph of the applicant.
6. Temporary resident card (INS Form I-688).
7. Employment authorization card (INS Form I-688A).

Applicants who don't have a List A document must provide *two* documents (one from List B and one from List C) to establish identity and employment eligibility. Such documents include:

1. State-issued driver's license or identification card containing a photograph.
2. School identification card with a photograph.
3. Voter registration card.
4. U.S. military card or draft record.
5. Identification card issued by federal, state, or local government agencies.
6. Military dependent identification card.
7. Native American tribal document.
8. U.S. Coast Guard merchant mariner card.
9. Driver's license issued by a Canadian government authority.

If the applicant is younger than 16 years old and cannot provide any of these documents, he or she can use the following to establish identity:

1. School record or report card.
2. Clinic or hospital record.
3. Daycare or nursery school record.

Minors can use these documents to establish employment eligibility:

1. Social security card (a copy or facsimile isn't acceptable).

2. An original or certified copy of a birth certificate issued by a state, county, or municipal authority bearing an official seal.
3. Unexpired INS employment authorization.
4. Unexpired reentry permit (INS Form I-327).
5. Unexpired refugee travel document (INS Form I-571).
6. Certification of birth issued by the Department of State (Form DS-1350).
7. U.S. identification card (INS Form I-197).
8. Native American tribal document.
9. Identification card for use of resident citizen in the United States (INS Form I-179).

It might be worthwhile to let prospective employees know that anyone who attempts to satisfy the employment eligibility requirements by using fraudulent identification or employment eligibility documents, or documents that were legally issued to another person, can receive a five-year prison term, a fine, or both.

IRCA and Discrimination

There's more to IRCA than having to check a lot of documents when taking on new employees. Under the act, an employer with four or more employees cannot discriminate in recruiting, hiring, or firing on the basis of an individual's national origin or, in the case of a citizen or would-be citizen, because of his or her citizenship status. IRCA's protection does not, of course, extend to unauthorized aliens.

IRCA doesn't cancel out Title VII of the Civil Rights Act of 1964, which also bans discrimination on the basis of national origin in recruitment, hiring, job assignments, firing, salary, and other terms and conditions of employment. Here's the difference: If an applicant works for a business with *15 or more* employees, he or she can file a national-origin discrimination suit under Title VII. But IRCA lets employees who work for businesses with *4 to 14* employees sue employers for discriminating on the grounds of national origin.

Under IRCA, an applicant or employee who wants to press charges of discrimination based on citizenship status against an employer with four or more employees, may do so with the Office of Special Counsel in the Department of Justice. The discrimination charges can be filed by an applicant who believes he or she lost out on an employment opportunity because of national origin or citizenship status, by a third party on the individual's behalf, or by INS officers who have reason to believe that discrimination has occurred. No matter who does the filing, discrimination charges must be filed within 180 days of the discriminatory act.

Within 10 days of receiving a charge of discrimination, the Office of Special Counsel will notify the employer by certified mail. After investigating the charge, the special counsel might file a complaint with an administrative law judge. If the special counsel does not file a complaint within 120 days of receiving the charge, the person making the charge can file a complaint with an administrative law judge, who will conduct a hearing and issue a decision.

If the judge determines that an employer has discriminated against an applicant because of his or her national origin, the employer will have to stop all discriminatory employment practices immediately. The judge may also order the employer to hire (with or without back pay) any individuals who might have been hurt by the discrimination and to pay a fine of up to $1,000 for each person discriminated against. (That figure can soar to $2,000 for employers with previous discrimination judgments.) If the judge decides that the losing party didn't have a reasonable basis for the claim, he or she may award attorneys' fees to the winner.

Stiff Penalties for IRCA Violations

If an employer does violate IRCA, the INS may decide to take civil action. An employer who knowingly hires illegal aliens, for instance, may have to pay some hefty fines:

- *First violation*: Not less than $250 and not more than $2,000 for each unauthorized employee.
- *Second violation*: Not less than $2,000 and not more than $5,000 for each unauthorized employee.
- *Subsequent violation*: Not less than $3,000 and not more than $10,000 for each unauthorized employee.

Also, employers who don't keep good records for the INS are asking for trouble. You must properly complete, retain, and present for inspection Form I-9 as demanded by law, or face civil fines as high as $1,000 for each employee for whom the form was not completed, retained, or presented. In determining penalties, the INS considers the size of your company, whether you made a good-faith effort to comply with the law, and whether the violation involved unauthorized employees.

Employers can't get away with making an applicant or employee pay a bond or indemnity in case the employer gets caught under IRCA. If the INS does find out, the employer automatically gets slapped with a $1,000 fine. In addition, the employer has to repay the bond money to the applicant or employee or, if that person can't be located, to the U.S. Treasury.

Sometimes IRCA offenses carry criminal as well as civil penalties. For instance, an employer who continuously and knowingly hires unauthorized aliens may have to pay fines of $3,000 per employee and/or serve six months in jail. Usually, the courts save these criminal sanctions for serious or repeat offenses.

CHECK THOSE REFERENCES

Considering what can happen if you don't do a reference check, it's astonishing how many employers don't bother. If they do check references, they barely scratch the surface. Prospective employers often explain their attitude toward reference checks by blaming uncooperative former employers: "They simply won't help you." Yes, you must deal with annoying privacy issues and other legal baggage in checking references ... but the alternative—*not* checking references—isn't even worth thinking about.

It's true that you might run the risk of a lawsuit from an unsuccessful job applicant if you step over the line in your reference checks. But you might run the risk of an even bigger and nastier lawsuit if the maladjusted employee whose references you didn't check harms or injures an innocent person.

Once you've decided you're going to take the plunge and do

thorough reference checks, these tips should help you stay on track:

1. Require all applicants to sign a release permitting you to contact references and stating that the references will be "held harmless" for whatever they say. See Figure 4–1 for a sample record release form.

2. Always check out a candidate's references *before* you make a formal offer of employment. After-the-fact reference checks can leave you wide open to a "wrongful discharge" suit from the applicant who accepted the job offer.

3. Carry out your reference checks as soon as possible to avoid possible litigation. Don't let applicants think they have a job waiting because they haven't heard from you. Also, keep in mind that you don't have to tell why an applicant didn't get a job or explain anything else about your hiring process.

4. If you decide not to hire an applicant because of negative references, relax. A litigious applicant will have to sue his or her former employer, not your company, for defamation of character, slander (false statements given in writing), or libel (false statements given orally, as over the phone). Also, it's up to the unsuccessful applicant to prove that the reference or the prospective employer's staff lied about him or her. The applicant will probably have a tough time showing in court that any defamatory or libelous act occurred.

Even if your reference checks aren't always successful, they can help if you hire an applicant and a third party sues you or if you turn an applicant down and he or she sues you on violation-of-privacy grounds. Hopefully you'll manage to stay out of court if you follow the advice in this book! If you do find yourself embroiled in a lawsuit, however, a thorough reference check will buttress your case. You'll need to show that you conducted more than a cursory reference check—that you made a conscientious effort to get all the facts, thereby meeting or exceeding industry practices. You'll also need to keep good records of your reference checks to refute any arguments that your actions were discriminatory or otherwise illegal.

You'll probably find that you don't have to do an extensive reference check for every applicant. When you do conduct reference checks, however, keep these things in mind:

1. Let the applicant know in advance whom you're going to contact, what you're going to ask about, and why you need the information.
2. Tell the applicant that the reference check may involve sensitive and highly personal areas of his or her life, depending on the job he or she is applying for. This warning should defuse any charges of discrimination in your hiring practices.
3. Do as thorough a check as you can to confirm the applicant's abilities and professional skills, and to verify his or her credentials.
4. When questioning a reference source for information about an applicant, stress that your questions are relevant to and important for the job the applicant is seeking.
5. Keep the tone of your questions to the reference source direct and professional. Avoid questions that might be construed as discriminatory.
6. If you conduct a credit check on an applicant as a means of verifying what his or her references have told you, be sure to notify the applicant in advance and have him or her sign a release.
7. Don't automatically assume that reference sources are a waste of time. Even if a reference lies to you about an applicant, you can generally read between the lines.

BACKGROUND CHECKS AND THE LAW

As is true of just about everything in hiring, you can do all the reference and background checks you want—as long as you don't violate any existing laws or regulations in the process.

An employer should always walk softly when gathering and processing information related to a job applicant. If the employer lands in court, it could well be because of the way in which he or she treated this sensitive information. But it's not hard to do the job right if you know which rules apply:

Regulations

At both the federal and local levels, there are numerous agencies that regulate various aspects of our economy. For instance, the Nuclear Regulatory Commission (NRC), which oversees the nuclear power industry, has set up guidelines for checking out the backgrounds and references of NRC job applicants. The U.S. Department of Transportation has similar background-checking guidelines for railroad and airline job applicants.

Constitutional Rights

All American citizens enjoy state and federal constitutional safeguards. One of the most important is that no one can deprive Americans of their privileges, immunities, and other legal rights. Depriving an individual of constitutionally guaranteed privacy rights, as we saw in Chapter 2, can mean big trouble for an employer.

The U.S. Supreme Court has interpreted the Constitution to give citizens the right to preserve the confidentiality of sensitive information in their personnel files. And Article I of the California state constitution guarantees citizens the right to "safety, happiness, and privacy." Six other states—Alaska, Arizona, Florida, Massachusetts, Montana, and Rhode Island—have similar privacy safeguards in their constitutions.

Statutes

A great many federal and state laws govern the manner and type of information employers can collect about job applicants in conducting background and reference checks. Unfortunately, these laws are in a constant state of flux, but that doesn't mean you should give up on learning about them. Be particularly careful to find out about local ordinances that regulate the types of information an employer can solicit from references and former employers.

Here are some other things you should be aware of in handling, processing, and maintaining the information obtained through background and reference checks:

Interdepartmental Exchanges. Although your organization may have several departments, don't let sensitive information such as medical records and personnel files flow freely among them. Take pains to protect the confidentiality of these records. A good rule of thumb is to treat an applicant's records with the same care you'd give the records of a current employee.

Requests from Unions. If a union requests information in an applicant's file, don't release it unless the union obtains the applicant's written consent first. Unions do have a special status under federal and state law, but that status doesn't entitle them to receive information on people who haven't been hired yet. Hold fast to this principle even if you've already offered the applicant a job.

Speaking of unions, keep in mind that if your company is a union shop, the labor agreement might restrict your preemployment checks. Failure to comply with this agreement could open your company to an investigation by the U.S. Department of Labor.

Your Fourth Amendment Rights. The Fourth Amendment to the U.S. Constitution prohibits "unreasonable searches and seizures." Unless government officials have a judicial or administrative subpoena, a search warrant, or a release from the applicant, you do not have to give up the applicant's files or records. It doesn't matter whether the request for the records was prompted by a criminal investigation or an EEOC inquiry into your company's hiring practices.

Criminal Records. Most people don't understand the difference between *arrest* and *conviction* records, but it's a crucial one in employment law: More than a dozen states prevent employers from using an arrest record in assessing an applicant unless that arrest resulted in a conviction or guilty plea.

The judicial reasoning here is that employers might use arrest records to discriminate against members of minority groups in hiring because they tend to be arrested more than people who aren't members of minority groups. The jurists who take this position say that employers should rely more heavily on *conviction* records, especially when evaluating applicants for sensitive jobs.

Even so, the applicant must be convicted of an offense that has something to do with the job he or she is seeking. For instance, an employer hiring account executives who spend most of their time on the road might pay attention to a DWI conviction. But a DWI conviction probably won't carry as much weight as a conviction for embezzlement if an unsuccessful applicant for a bank job goes to court.

Private Verification Firms. If you retain the services of a private verification firm to check an applicant's background and references, remember that your company can be sued if the firm slips up. After all, the investigative firm is only an outside consultant acting as your agent. You can outline the firm's responsibilities in writing, but that probably won't be enough to get you completely off the hook in court. You might still be liable for negligence for illegal acts committed by the verification firm.

Impersonations. Some employers are frustrated actors: They like to impersonate others when contacting reference sources provided by an applicant. If the source of the information is, say, a worker at a federal agency, he or she can take legal action against the employer under certain conditions. But the applicant can't do anything about it unless he or she can demonstrate malice or some other outrageous act on the part of the employer.

Employers need to take background checks much more seriously than they currently do. Background and reference checks weed out quacks, fakes, and unauthorized workers. They help you zero in on dangerous individuals who might threaten the health and safety of others. And, of course, they identify the highest-quality applicants.

I think the best advice I can give you is to follow this guideline:

**It's smarter to do background and reference checks
than not to do them, as long as you don't
violate any laws.**

CHAPTER 5

TO TEST OR NOT TO TEST

Testing is one of the toughest employment-related dilemmas of our time: It pits a job applicant's privacy rights against a prospective employer's right to compete effectively in the marketplace. Both claim that truth, justice, and the American way are on their side. Who's right?

More and more employers are turning to testing as a way of weeding out unqualified and undesirable employees from the work force. The result, unfortunately, seems to be more and more lawsuits, both from prospective employees and those who are already on board:

• Alex S. applied for a computer programming position with a big New York bank and was asked to undergo drug testing. He did so willingly; he didn't do drugs and had nothing to hide. Needless to say, he was surprised to learn that he had tested positive. When Alex tried to explain that he had been taking a painkiller prescribed by his doctor, the bank's personnel interviewer snapped, "We run a drug-free workplace." That was the end of the interview, and a less qualified applicant got the programming job.

• When Jim D. applied for a more responsible job at the insurance company where he worked, the personnel office asked him to take a polygraph (lie-detector) test. Anxious to get the job, he consented. Jim felt that the interviews had gone well and that the job was in the bag. Two weeks later, however, he was told that the position was no longer available. Although he could not prove anything, he was sure that the results of his polygraph exam had something to do with losing the job: As a teenager, Jim had had a few brushes with the law, and the polygraph examiner had asked questions about previous arrests.

• Marian J., a recent college graduate, applied for a sales job with a major retail chain. During her interview, she was asked to take an honesty test but was not told why such a test was necessary. Without giving the matter much thought, she took the test. Several weeks passed without word from her prospective employer. She finally phoned the personnel office only to discover that the position had been filled. When Marian talked to a friend who worked for the company, the friend confided that Marian had not scored well on the honesty test.

These situations are not unique or unusual. In fact, they're becoming the norm as employers across the United States spend millions of dollars each day to test both prospective *and* current employees for everything from drug use to honesty to genetic markers.

The testing mania has spawned a new industry of vendors— a dime-a-dozen crew of drug labs, honesty-testing firms, and security consultants who are happy to take your money for testing job applicants and current employees. Likewise, testing has attracted an army of lawyers in search of hot new markets, such as the millions of angry job applicants and employees who would love to take you to court because of testing procedures they consider unfair.

When an applicant does sue a potential employer over testing, the employer often loses. If you don't believe me, take another look at what could have happened in the three examples I gave earlier:

• Alex S.: It's common practice for employers who do drug testing to give someone who tests positive the option to retest or at least to offer an explanation for the test results—as Alex attempted to do. After the personnel interviewer cut him short, Alex could have filed a complaint with his local human rights commission or even explored the possibility of suing the bank, especially if its personnel guidelines included provisions for retesting. Moreover, if Alex were a member of a minority group, he would be able to call on federal and state civil rights laws to sue the bank for possibly using drug tests to discriminate in hiring.

• Jim D.: Lie-detector tests are strictly regulated at both the federal and state levels. Under most of the present regulations, polygraph exams must be voluntary and must not affect an employer's decision to hire or promote someone. (I'll go into detail on these restrictions later in this chapter.) For now, it's enough to say that if Jim had consulted an attorney about the lie-detector test, the insurance company would have been on the receiving end of a lawsuit. And it would have faced penalties and fines from the U.S. Department of Labor.

• Marian J.: A growing number of states view honesty tests as "paper polygraphs" and regulate them in the same way as lie-detector exams. New York and other states forbid honesty-test questions that delve into a potential employee's arrest history, political convictions, or religious beliefs. Rhode Island, Massachusetts, and other states require that an applicant be told in advance what the intended use of the honesty test will be; at that point, the applicant must be given the option not to take the test. Also, the applicant's refusal to take the test can't influence the employer's hiring decision.

Marian could have taken legal action, especially because the retail chain failed to explain the purpose of the test to her. If it turned out that test results influenced the hiring decision in any way and Marian opted to take the case to court, the chain would probably find itself in thousands of dollars of trouble.

THE RIGHT TO TEST

While under the influence of drugs, an airline ticket agent assaults and seriously injures a passenger at New York's Kennedy Airport. A hotel maid in San Francisco, angry at her supervisor, starts a fire in the hotel lobby; several guests have to be hospitalized. A Boston hospital orderly with a long history of psychiatric problems stabs an elderly patient.

The news reminds us daily that cases like these are all too common. What it doesn't tell us is that the stories don't end with the employee's arrest and possible conviction. In all three cases, the *employer* also faces a multimillion dollar judgment.

It's a truism of employment law that employers are liable for the acts of their employees. You have a duty to make sure that people who aren't suited for the job aren't hired and that those who manage to slip through the hiring net aren't kept on. To protect the health and safety of both the work force and the public, you may need to resort to testing. If you don't want your testing program to backfire on you, however, you need to understand the legal framework in which testing operates.

General Duty

Employers have a legal responsibility to make sure that their employees don't harm or injure themselves or their co-workers. This widely accepted principle is called the "general duty doctrine." If you want to do your general duty, you have a legal obligation to test all prospective employees, to discipline or fire employees who refuse to undergo testing, to maintain discipline and promote safety in the workplace through proper testing, and to use tests to ensure that employees improve their job-related skills.

But the general duty doctrine does not give you the right to use tests to find out about an employee's or job applicant's political, religious, or sexual preferences; social activities or associations; arrest records (unless specifically required by law, as in a regulated industry); or medical history (unless it has a direct bearing on the job in question).

Workplace Safety

Employers also have a legal responsibility to eliminate foreseeable or preventable hazards from the work environment. The Occupational Safety and Health Act of 1970 (OSHA) reflects the federal government's efforts to ensure that the work environment is free from hazards that could endanger the health and safety of employees or the public.

OSHA authorizes the federal government to establish mandatory guidelines for protecting workplace health and safety. Similar legislation exists at the state level.

Although OSHA doesn't give an applicant or employee the right to take sweeping legal action against an employer, it does allow members of the public to ask that the government investigate a particular workplace to determine whether it complies with federal health and safety guidelines. If it doesn't, the government has the authority to make the employer correct any problems.

OSHA and its state counterparts don't directly support the right of employers to test their job applicants and employees. Backed up by the general duty doctrine, however, OSHA laws establish the *need* to test. Furthermore, both OSHA and the general duty doctrine lend support to the argument that employers ensure that employees pose no threat to their co-workers or to innocent third parties. If you use employee testing as a means to fulfill this obligation, you're on solid legal ground.

Contractual Obligations

Because the employment relationship is a contractual one, as explained in Chapter 1, an employer can make testing a condition of hiring or continued employment. Under the "contract" stipulated by the at-will doctrine, the courts allow you to test applicants and employees—as long as the testing follows all relevant laws and guidelines.

A given of this employer-employee contract is that both sides deal fairly and honestly with each other. Thus, you can use testing as a legitimate vehicle for culling out unqualified and poorly trained employees. To fulfill the contract, however, be sure to let applicants and employees know what you're doing and why you're doing it.

The employment relationship is a two-way street: Just as employers can hire anyone they want (within the limits I've described, of course), employees can work for whomever they want. As the courts see it, job applicants and current employees *do* have a choice about testing: They can "vote with their feet" and look for work somewhere else if they don't want to be tested.

Right to Supervise

You have a legal obligation to supervise your employees properly. Testing is one way of making sure that workers comply with an organization's rules and regulations.

The lie detector has turned up frequently in internal investigations to identify employees who violate established work rules. Psychological tests have been used to identify employees with a tendency toward certain disorders or problems. And testing for honesty has become widespread as a means of curbing theft and other misuses of an employer's property by members of the work force.

But even testing to satisfy an established legal principle such as the right to supervise can leave you vulnerable to attack. To avoid hassles, you must monitor and fine-tune these aspects of your testing program:

Coercion. Applicants, employees, and other "outsiders" must not see the testing as coercive or unjust. Labor unions often complain that honesty tests are really given to intimidate employees and to influence union membership and decisions. To withstand a legal challenge, testing must comply with any collective bargaining agreements that may be in effect. Such agreements usually restrain the way in which employers can use lie-detector tests in disciplinary actions against employees.

Quality. The quality and accuracy of the tests an employer uses are bound to come up in court. For instance, congressional critics of truth tests have noted that it's nearly impossible to use a 15-minute polygraph examination to predict with any degree of certainty whether an employee has violated work rules.

Training. The courts also carefully scrutinize the training and experience of the individual who administers the tests. Many applicants and employees complain that employers hire poorly trained examiners in an attempt to cut costs.

Methods. A company recently lost a case because one of its polygraph examiners asked a female employee questions about her sex life. If you want to win, keep tabs on the tester's methods and manner. And take special care that the testing is not abusive or degrading because such tactics leave the employer open to violation-of-privacy and discrimination lawsuits.

Frequency.   How often you test can get you into trouble as well. Too many tests can seem like discrimination to the regulators, particularly if they zero in on members of a specific racial, ethnic, or religious group. Likewise, if you have one person undergo too many tests, the regulators might think you're targeting that person for persecution or punishment.

Basically, you do have the right to use testing to supervise or discipline your work force, but this testing must comply with the federal and state laws currently regulating the testing procedures you select. For instance, you can use AIDS testing as a supervisory tool if a job involves physical labor, but the testing must conform to local ordinances and laws.

Relationship to the Job

All acts by employers toward employees must have some link or "nexus" to the job, and testing is no exception. If you're going to test potential or current employees, you'd better make sure that the tests have something to do with the job in question.

The courts occasionally break this rule, but only if the public interest is at stake and the consequences would be disastrous. If a prospective employee will have access to money or drugs, for instance, the courts give you laissez-faire to test for tendencies to commit criminal acts. Also, the courts will generally let you conduct drug or alcohol tests on individuals who work as security guards or in other positions directly involving public safety. Judges, like the rest of us, have no desire to be on a bus or airplane operated by someone who is drunk or stoned.

Mandatory Testing

In some situations, an employer can't really do much about the testing procedure or the type and frequency of tests to be administered. Polygraph exams are strictly regulated in the private sector, for example, but U.S. Department of Defense contractors use them freely during preemployment and for in-house disciplinary purposes.

The decision to test or not to test applicants and employees is often outside an employer's control. Testing may be mandated by federal or state regulations—and employers may be penalized if they fail to test.

In the banking industry, honesty examinations are a way of life. Federal regulators actually encourage their use, especially in the present climate of bank frauds and failures. The same holds true for the pharmaceutical industry, where the U.S. Drug Enforcement Administration (DEA) keeps a tight rein on the handling of controlled substances. The DEA encourages pharmaceutical companies to test their employees for drug use, and also indirectly promotes the use of honesty testing.

Discrimination

As is true of everything else in the workplace, testing cannot violate federal and state antidiscrimination regulations. The courts consider race, national origin, religion, politics, and sex as taboo areas in testing. Because the U.S. Constitution protects an individual's freedom of worship, association, and political belief, what an employee does outside the workplace is his or her own business.

A test cannot appear to discriminate against a particular person or group of people, as I said earlier. By extension, a test cannot attempt to influence the legitimate activities of workers or labor unions.

Labor unions and employers have been at each other's throats in the United States for more than a century. Not surprisingly, many labor leaders take a dim view of the American employer's right to test prospective and current employees. In fact, labor union concern that tests have become subtle means of discouraging workers from union activity has prompted some of the recent federal and state legislation to regulate testing.

Legal skirmishes between unions and employers can also lead to federal investigations. The National Labor Relations Board and the EEOC have stated that employers cannot use testing to interfere with employees' freedom to unionize and exercise their rights. Honesty examinations, in particular, have struck a sour note with the unions. So, if you want to save money and avoid a time-consuming government investigation, make sure your testing procedures don't rile any unions! Be especially careful if your company has one of the 250,000-plus collective bargaining agreements in the United States.

Business Environment

Whether or not you test applicants and employees depends on the business environment in which you operate. Business needs will likely shape your testing procedures and policies.

An ongoing concern in the information industry is protecting data, so the honesty of prospective and current employees is paramount. And in the international sphere, some countries are so concerned about the spread of AIDS that they require employees of U.S. corporations to be tested for the virus before being granted work permits. Such countries include Singapore, Saudi Arabia, the People's Republic of China, Hong Kong, and Japan.

WHERE THE LAW STANDS

Employers often violate testing laws—not because they give illegal tests but because of the *manner* in which they test. The rules and regulations that govern testing are pretty thorny, but if you're not constantly alert to changes in the law, you could run into some even thornier legal hassles.

Drug Testing

Probably no area of employee testing is more controversial or complicated than drug screening. New federal, state, and local legislative developments that affect drug testing seem to crop up every day. And the states may have a very different attitude from the federal government. (See Table 5–1.)

Sadly, there's a real need for drug testing in the American workplace. According to the U.S. Department of Justice, Americans are responsible for more than half of the world's illegal drug use. Here are some sobering statistics on drugs:

- Sixty-five percent of all persons entering the work force for the first time have used illicit drugs.

TABLE 5–1
How the States View Drug Testing

State	Drug Testing Laws
Iowa	Prohibit applicant testing unless test given as part of preemployment physical Require employer to use services of state-approved lab Require confirming test for all positive results Require employer to give applicant reasonable opportunity to rebut or explain test results Treat employer violations of law as simple misdemeanors
Minnesota	Regulate applicant testing Permit applicants to sue for damages, including attorney's fees
Montana	Restrict applicant testing Treat violations as misdemeanors
Rhode Island	Prohibit direct observation of urine specimen collection and testing Require reasonable grounds before current employees can be tested Treat violations as misdemeanors
Utah	Legalize private-sector drug testing for any reason as long as policy is established and distributed in writing Do not consider false test results grounds for litigation if employer's reliance on results was reasonable and in good faith
Vermont	Restrict applicant testing Permit applicant or employee to bring civil suit for damages Treat violations as misdemeanors

- As many as 23 percent of all U.S. workers use dangerous drugs *on the job.*
- More than 20 million workers use marijuana on a regular basis (at least four times a month), and more than 5 million workers are regular cocaine users.

- More than 500,000 U.S. employees are addicted to heroin, and more than 10 million use pharmaceuticals without a prescription.

The cost of drug use in the workplace shows up in high absenteeism, reduced productivity, theft and vandalism of employer property, dramatic increase in on-the-job accidents, and high employee turnover. The U.S. Chamber of Commerce says that drug abuse in the workplace costs American employers more than $80 billion annually, with more than $35 billion of that amount going down the drain in lost productivity.

Under existing laws, private employers have both a right and an obligation to test employees for drugs. In an effort to comply, many employers have developed education, training, and testing programs, often under the same umbrella.

Even though drug testing is perfectly legal, it can get you into hot water if you don't handle and monitor it properly. In rulings over the last decade, the courts have laid out the following guidelines:

1. Preemployment and "for cause" drug testing are generally all right, but "random" drug testing is *not* acceptable, especially if random tests appear to target a particular population in the work force.
2. Quality control is the name of the game in drug testing. You must make sure that test samples are kept under lock and key, and that only properly trained personnel do the tests. Make sure testing, collection, and handling procedures are reliable and accurate, and take steps to prevent false or incorrect identification of samples and results.
3. To remove your company's legal liability, you should ask prospective and current employees who are to be tested to sign a waiver form. You need to clearly explain the waiver to the person undergoing the test, and ensure that he or she signs it voluntarily. *Never* put any pressure on an applicant or employee to submit to drug testing!
4. Your testing procedures should be fair and consistent with company policies; you must treat all employees who have positive test results the same, no matter what position they hold. If the company has a collective bargaining

agreement, the testing program must be in line with its provisions.

5. You must treat the results of any drug test as confidential and release them only to authorized personnel. Many states consider drug test results to be medical records, so employers must handle them accordingly.

6. You should give applicants and employees who test positive the first time around an opportunity to explain the results, and then offer them the option to retest. If a current employee tests positive or openly admits to having a drug problem, you might consider providing access to counseling or other forms of help through an employee assistance program.

The kind of drug testing program you implement will depend on your needs and resources:

Preemployment. Job applicants are by far the largest group currently being tested for drug use. Virtually all employers who test for drugs do so at the preemployment stage. Because you can make being "drug free" a condition for employment, a job applicant doesn't have much choice about cooperating if he or she wants the job.

Unlike drug testing for current employees, testing for job applicants is not complicated by union contracts, job performance questions, pensions, severance pay, and grievance procedures. Moreover, many employers consider testing at the preemployment stage the most cost-effective method since it helps keep drug abusers off the payroll.

Safety. From a legal standpoint, testing employees involved in jobs where the safety of co-workers and the public is at stake is easily justified. The courts have made it clear that the security of the public cannot be compromised, even at the risk of compromising the privacy of an employee. Public safety is, or should be, the top priority in any business.

Not testing employees and applicants as a safety precaution can mean expensive litigation if a worker on drugs injures an innocent third party. Subway conductors, bulldozer operators, and airline pilots are logical candidates for such testing because they hold the safety of others in their hands.

Security. Employers have a legal right to take all "reasonable and prudent" steps to protect their assets and property. That's why the courts have consistently upheld drug testing in industries where employees handle large amounts of money or other valuables.

"For Cause." Testing for cause is a common element in investigations after accidents in which human error by an employee may have harmed or injured others. You can also test if a specific event strongly indicates that an employee has a drug problem or has been observed bringing illegal drugs on company premises.

Posttreatment. An employer has a right to ask employees who have participated in a drug rehabilitation program to be retested. Continued employment may depend on the results of posttreatment tests, and failure to submit to retesting may be sufficient grounds for dismissal or denial of the former job.

Routine. Except for preemployment tests, most employee drug testing takes place as part of routine medical examinations, such as a required annual physical. This is especially true for employees involved in high-stress positions or jobs requiring physical endurance.

Random. As I said before, random drug tests are controversial. In fact, they're responsible for most of the litigation involving drug testing.

Employees view random, unannounced drug testing as arbitrary and offensive. Such tests are likely to trigger labor union grievances, and they're also the most difficult to defend in court. I wouldn't recommend random drug screening, but if you decide to do it for any reason, read up on the applicable laws first.

No matter how or why you test your prospective and current employees, you should follow these general guidelines to prevent lawsuits:

1. Don't use drug testing to discipline employees for unrelated reasons, such as absenteeism or poor performance on the job.
2. Never target any specific group of individuals for testing, especially members of a group protected by law.
3. Never limit the testing only to lower-level employees. Not only can this weaken your legal basis for testing, but it may destroy your employees' confidence in the testing program.
4. Put the testing policy in writing, and communicate it to all employees. (No personnel policy should ever be only verbal.)
5. Avoid acting on the results of one test. Always confirm a positive test result with a second test. (Retesting job applicants may not be necessary unless the applicant has a plausible explanation for the positive results.)
6. If a union gets involved, don't refuse to talk about drug testing with it. The National Labor Relations Act requires employers to bargain with unions about *all* conditions related to employment, not just wages.

Alcohol Testing

Alcohol use isn't just legal; it's an almost universal part of American life—perhaps a little too universal. More than 12 million Americans are alcoholics, and another 90 to 100 million are social drinkers who consume alcohol at least once a week.

Although drug abuse has captured the attention of the media, government, and public, the number one problem at the workplace continues to be alcohol:

- Absenteeism among problem drinkers is as much as 8.3 times greater than the normal figure for employees, according to the Employee Assistance Society of North America. Also, alcohol abuse substantially affects the quality and amount of work that employees perform.
- Alcohol abuse costs employers more than $65 billion annually in lost productivity, which is nearly twice the cost of decreased productivity caused by the abuse of

all other drugs combined, according to the Research Triangle Institute.

- Up to 40 percent of all industrial fatalities are connected to alcohol in the workplace, and more than 45 percent of all on-the-job injuries are related to alcohol.
- Alcohol abuse costs employers billions of dollars in health care every year. The National Institute of Alcoholism and Alcohol Abuse says that an alcoholic employee undergoing treatment can cost his or her employer more than $1,000 per month.

In today's workplace, you not only have to be concerned about the rising costs associated with alcoholic employees, but also about how the courts are treating the liability of employers for the acts of their workers, both on and off the job. This liability is costing employers millions of dollars in legal and court fees.

Under the employment laws of the past, employers had no obligation to control the behavior of their employees, let alone their drinking habits. This was especially true for things workers did outside the workplace. But the situation has changed dramatically within the last 10 years, thanks largely to the efforts of grassroots groups such as Mothers Against Drunk Driving.

Legally, this 180-degree reversal can be traced to a seminal court case in 1983: The Texas Supreme Court held the Otis Elevator Company liable for a fatal accident involving one of its employees. The court ruled that Otis had not done enough to prevent drinking on the job. Even though the accident didn't happen at the Otis facility, the court said that it occurred because Otis had failed to take appropriate action to stop employee drinking on company premises.

Now that other states are following the Otis ruling, you have a bigger responsibility than ever before to curtail applicant and employee drinking. You cannot contribute to or condone drinking at the workplace; in fact, you're supposed to discourage it. Although you're not expected to act as a police officer, you *are* expected to identify problem drinkers and do whatever is necessary to ensure that they don't pose a threat to their co-workers or the public. If this means getting the drinker into a treatment program, so be it.

Under traditional employment law, employers didn't have to

discipline or fire employees who drank on the job. But now the courts permit and even support these punitive measures.

The legal rationale and conditions for alcohol testing are pretty much the same as those for drug testing. If an employer has a "reasonable basis" to test for alcohol use and abuse, the courts will uphold the testing process and results in a legal battle as long as the tests are fair and nondiscriminatory. A "reasonable basis" might be a supervisor observing an employee drinking on company premises or working while obviously under the influence of alcohol.

According to the at-will doctrine, you can require job applicants to submit to alcohol testing as a condition for employment. However, you must watch how you go about it.

The Federal Rehabilitation Act of 1973 prohibits employers from discriminating against the handicapped in hiring or firing. Drug and alcohol abuse are considered handicaps, so the act gives legal rights to substance abusers unless their use of drugs or alcohol affects their job performance or presents a danger to the abuser and the public.

Specifically, the act prohibits employers from:

1. Refusing to hire job applicants because they have a history of drug or alcohol abuse.
2. Asking a job applicant if he or she has ever abused drugs or alcohol.
3. Using the results of a drug or alcohol test to discriminate against a qualified handicapped individual.
4. Passing over a handicapped person for promotion, training, or salary increase because he or she refuses to be tested.

The Rehabilitation Act doesn't demand that an employer hire applicants with positive drug or alcohol test results. It simply requires employers not to discriminate against applicants with handicaps—and drug and alcohol abusers can qualify as handicapped persons.

As noted in Chapter 1, the Rehabilitation Act has a limited reach: It applies only to contractors or subcontractors who receive $2,500 or more in federal contracts, and to employers who receive federal financial assistance such as research grants or Small

Business Administration loans. Private-sector employers probably don't have to worry about the act's applicability to their drug and alcohol testing programs.

Contagious Diseases

Until AIDS became a global pandemic, neither the courts nor the public paid much attention to the testing of employees and job applicants for contagious diseases. AIDS has changed that feeling to the point where the term *employee testing* has become synonymous with AIDS testing.

The courts have traditionally upheld the testing of employees and job applicants for tuberculosis, venereal disease, and similar illnesses that can be spread to co-workers and the public. But AIDS poses special problems. Unlike most of these diseases, AIDS is lethal:

- According to the New York Business Group on Health, more than 179,000 Americans will die of AIDS by 1991, and almost all of them will be members of America's work force.
- AIDS costs employers more than $50 billion a year in lost productivity, rising medical insurance premiums, and disability pay.
- The Risk Management Society has said that AIDS will affect every employer in the United States by the 1990s.

Whether the disease is AIDS or tuberculosis, you do have a right to test employees for it. Of course, the testing must be voluntary. And, as always, it must not be discriminatory or single out any specific group of individuals—including homosexual men.

The fact that an employee tests positive for AIDS is no longer grounds for termination. The courts and legislatures now expect you to approach the problem from a rehabilitation standpoint. Possible courses of action include:

1. Arranging for the person with AIDS (PWA) to work at home.
2. Implementing special hygiene conditions to protect the health and safety of co-workers and the public.

3. Rearranging the work area or the employee's work schedule.
4. Letting the employee take a leave of absence.
5. Helping the employee identify public and private sources of assistance outside the company.

If a prospective or current employee does take a test for contagious diseases, you must follow these guidelines:

1. Ensure that only reputable laboratories handle the testing.
2. Ensure that the test results are kept confidential and released only to authorized persons.
3. Ensure that the testing procedures are fair, nondiscriminatory, and related to the job in question.
4. Ensure that testing procedures comply with both federal and state laws.

You can make AIDS testing a condition for employment unless local laws forbid it. But you must never coerce, pressure, or force an employee or job applicant to be tested for AIDS.

At this writing, the federal courts have not expanded the Rehabilitation Act of 1973 to cover PWAs. Advocates are arguing, however, that if a person has AIDS or another terminal illness, he or she is handicapped and should therefore be covered by the act. If the Rehabilitation Act were to extend to AIDS and other contagious diseases, you would have to treat PWAs the same as you now do drug and alcohol abusers in hiring and firing (providing, of course, that the Rehabilitation Act applied to your business).

No matter what the federal courts decide, you still have an obligation to protect the safety and health of your employees and the public. That means you have the right to test for contagious diseases, as long as you handle the testing properly and are on the alert for any hint of discrimination.

Lie-Detector Tests

The late Senator Sam Ervin called lie-detector tests "20th-century witchcraft, " but for the last 50 years, employers have sworn by them in industries such as retailing, precious metals, hotels, and banking. Until the Federal Employee Polygraph Protection

Act was passed in 1988, employers administered more than 2 million lie-detector tests to prospective and current employees each year.

Many of these employers were convinced that lie-detector tests helped cut losses due to employee crime. One hotel chain reported to Congress that lie-detector testing had cut back its losses from theft by over $1 million annually in the chain's Atlanta hotel alone.

Even if you believe that lie-detector tests tell the gospel truth, you can't use them however and whenever you see fit. Now that the federal government has gotten in on the act, you need to understand the limitations that the law imposes. Failure to comply with these regulations could result in fines of more than $10,000 per incident under the Polygraph Act.

The act defines "lie detector" to include polygraph machines, voice-stress analyzers, deceptographs, psychological stress evaluators, and all other mechanical or electrical devices that can render an opinion about the honesty of an employee or job applicant.

Under the act, no employer engaged in interstate commerce can demand that an employee or job applicant submit to lie-detector testing. You cannot discharge, discipline, refuse to hire, or discriminate in any way against an individual who refuses to take a lie-detector test, or who complains or takes legal action under the act.

The Polygraph Act gives the Labor Department authority to regulate lie-detector tests. The department can conduct investigations, file civil lawsuits against violators, and impose sanctions and fines. Job applicants and employees who have grievances file their complaints with the department. If you violate the act, you are liable to the prospective or current employee affected by the violations. Restitution can range from employment or reinstatement, to promotion or payment of lost wages and benefits.

The U.S. government, state and local governments, and their subdivisions are exempt from the act's coverage. Likewise, the act does not apply to federal contractors engaged in national security work; companies providing private security services, including guard companies, armored-car services, and alarm firms; or employers involved in manufacturing, distributing, or dispensing controlled substances.

The act *does* permit the use of lie-detector examinations for internal criminal investigations if the employer has reasonable basis to suspect an employee of embezzlement, theft, industrial espionage, sabotage, or drug use. If an employee takes a lie-detector test for an internal investigation, the examiner cannot ask the employee about his or her religious beliefs, opinions on racial matters, political beliefs or affiliations, sexual behavior, or beliefs or activities involving labor unions.

Before the test, you must tell the applicant or employee in writing about:

1. The date, time, and location of the test.
2. The nature and characteristics of the test and the type of testing instrument that will be used.
3. The right of the applicant or employee to consult with an attorney or union representative before the test.

You must also tell job applicants that taking the test is not a condition for employment, and describe the applicant's rights in case the examination violates the Polygraph Act.

To ensure that only properly trained and qualified examiners conduct lie-detector tests, the act requires that an examiner have a valid license from the state in which the test is being conducted, maintain a minimum of $50,000 bond or the equivalent amount of professional liability coverage, keep all test records for at least three years, and not disclose the test results to anyone except the examinee and the employer who ordered the test.

Thirty states also regulate the use of lie-detector tests. Companies that operate only within one city, county, or state would have to comply with the regulations of the state in which they do their business.

The state regulations echo the provisions of the federal act in many ways. In general, they require that employers use only examiners licensed in the state where the test is conducted. As always, the testing must be voluntary. An attorney or union representative can accompany the applicant or employee to the test. The examiner cannot ask about the prospective or current employee's religious or political beliefs or sex life, and the examination cannot be discriminatory or anti-union. If the examiner asks offensive questions, the examinee doesn't have to answer them. He or she must also have an opportunity to explain any answers.

Unlike federal regulations, however, state laws permit employers to refuse employment to job applicants who refuse to take a lie-detector test.

If you're thinking about using lie-detector tests, check out the guidelines for your state first. In many states, the state police or a specifically designated polygraph board is responsible for enforcing polygraph regulations. You should educate yourself about your local and state laws before implementing any kind of lie-detector policy in your company.

Honesty Tests

Now that the Federal Employee Polygraph Protection Act has restricted the use of lie-detector examinations, a growing number of employers are turning to paper-and-pencil honesty tests. Like their mechanical and electronic counterparts, these tests are designed to probe for dishonest tendencies in employees and job applicants.

At present, there are no federal regulations for honesty tests as there are for lie-detector exams although this will probably change in the future. But some states have started to regulate honesty testing.

In general, state regulations say that an employer cannot target any specific group of individuals for honesty testing. Honesty tests must avoid questions that infringe on the employee's right to privacy, freedom of association or religion, political beliefs, or union activities. And they cannot raise questions about past arrests, juvenile criminal records, and drug abuse history.

Honesty tests are inexpensive and usually less offensive than lie-detector exams. They've become popular with hotel chains, clothing retailers, convenience stores, and other businesses where employees regularly handle money, merchandise, or valuables. Because honesty tests have come under fire in recent years, however, you shouldn't base your hiring decisions solely on honesty testing. Look at the honesty test results in conjunction with other yardsticks of performance and behavior.

Psychological Tests

Psychological tests come in many varieties and evaluate many different characteristics. There are old standbys such as the Minnesota Multiphasic Personality Inventory, which psychologists have been using to assess personality traits for many years. There are also personality-profile exams that measure an applicant's interests and aptitudes, and tests that claim to gauge patience, aggressive tendencies, and adaptability to changing environments.

Psychological tests, like honesty tests, have been sharply criticized, especially by some minority leaders. But the courts have consistently upheld their legality. Unless an applicant can prove that a psychological examination is discriminatory, it's highly unlikely that the courts will say anything about it.

Genetic Screening

It may sound like something out of *Brave New World*, but some companies are starting to examine applicants' tissue samples for particular genetic markers or characteristics. The proponents of genetic screening claim that it will help employers cut down on medical insurance costs and raise productivity by identifying applicants with a predisposition toward certain problems. But its critics charge that genetic screening can give employers a powerful discriminatory weapon to use against some groups in American society, particularly as the technology becomes more refined.

There are currently no federal or state regulations for genetic screening, probably because it's so new. At present, you can do genetic screening as long as the testing is nondiscriminatory, the test results are confidential, and only reputable laboratories are used.

Over the last few years, Congress has been taking a hard look at genetic testing, and several bills have made their way to the legislature. Capitol Hill insiders predict that it is only a matter of time before the government imposes some restrictions, especially if the labor unions press for regulation or employers abuse the test procedures and results.

TESTING TIPS

The need to test is unfortunate, but there doesn't seem to be much that employers can do about it. One thing is becoming crystal clear: In the next decade, more and more employers will have to test more and more workers, before and after they come on board. The guidelines given in this chapter should help you understand the who, when, why, and how of testing. But even if you can't keep track of all the legal details, these three rules should point you in the right direction—away from court:

**Do not discriminate in testing or give
the appearance of discrimination.**

**Become knowledgeable about the regulations
and laws that govern your particular situation,
and be aware of potential changes in the law.**

**Ensure that your testing methods, procedures, and
administrators are of the highest quality.**

CHAPTER 6

INTERVIEW INS AND OUTS

Although testing garners more media attention, interviewing can be just as much of a legal minefield for employers. A substantial number of the employment-related cases currently before the courts involve statements made by employers during the interviewing process—some in jest, others in ignorance. The point is that loose lips can cost employers a lot of money:

• Veronica J. applied for a management position with a high-tech consulting firm in Connecticut. After completing a series of aptitude and psychological tests, as well as undergoing an extensive background check, Veronica was certain that the job was hers. Then the question of her pregnancy came up. "How long have you been pregnant?" the interviewer asked. "Three months, " Veronica answered. The interviewer commented, "You certainly don't look it, " and went on to finish the interview. When Veronica didn't get the job, she filed a complaint with the EEOC.

• Abdul S., a Pakistani with a permanent resident alien visa, applied for a job with a retail chain in New Jersey. During Abdul's interview, the personnel manager asked him about his religious preferences. "Why do you want to know?" Abdul asked. "No reason, " the interviewer responded. Abdul didn't get the job, so he sued the retail chain. The jury awarded him $241,500 in damages.

• When Richard L., a 58-year-old accountant, applied for a position with a large Los Angeles bank, the personnel interviewer casually asked him, "How does it feel to get older?" Richard didn't answer. After several weeks went by, he phoned the bank to ask about his application. The personnel office told him that the bank had offered the job to a younger man, but said that age hadn't played a part in the decision. Nonetheless, Richard filed an age discrimination complaint with the Los Angeles human rights commission.

Your mouth *can* get you into trouble if you ask the wrong interview questions or if you ask the right ones in the wrong context. The appearance of impropriety can cost you as much as impropriety itself. But the guidelines set forth in this chapter should help you avoid some of the most common legal problems associated with interviewing.

WHAT TO AVOID

In general, an interview must not:

1. Try to elicit personal information about an applicant simply for the purpose of finding reasons not to hire him or her.
2. Seek to determine his or her political or religious beliefs or to learn how he or she feels about labor unions.
3. Attempt to get the applicant to divulge a former employer's trade secrets, especially if the former employer is a competitor.

A swarm of federal and local regulations govern the hiring process, and interviews are no exception. (I'll go into more detail about the regulators in the next chapter.) These regulations extend even to seemingly innocuous statements and "jokes" made during interviews. If a job applicant is a member of a group protected under Title VII (minorities, women, older people, etc.), he or she could easily misinterpret such statements. Therefore, you should walk on eggs when you talk about any of the following areas with a prospective employee.

Sex

A job applicant's sex life is none of your business. Some states even have laws banning interview questions about an applicant's sexual preferences, mores, or behavior.

As mentioned in Chapter 1, Title VII does not protect homosexuals from discrimination in employment although some states have passed gay rights acts that do. Actually, Title VII does not specifically address whether an employer can ask questions about an applicant's sexual preferences. But it does prohibit sexual harassment of female applicants and employees—and questions about a woman's sex life could certainly be construed as a form of harassment.

Marital Status

There are some state and local laws that limit the questions you can ask about an applicant's marital status, but neither the courts nor the legislatures have had the last word on this issue yet. The best tactic is to avoid questions about marriage, cohabitation, and so on.

In cases where you really need this information, you should ask both male and female applicants the same questions. Obviously, you should also avoid any inquiries that might sound sexist.

Health

Unless the applicant has a physical or mental disability that could affect his or her job performance, you should steer clear of health-related questions. In cases where an applicant's health would affect his or her ability to do the job, make sure your questions and comments relate directly to the job or work environment.

Physique

Although Title VII doesn't cover questions about an applicant's physical size or weight, don't use these variables as hiring criteria unless they have something to do with the job. The courts and regulators tend to view inquiries about physique as discriminatory, especially if the questions are directed at female or minority applicants.

Religion

Remember the old warning about not discussing religion or politics at cocktail parties? Well, they're also good subjects to stay away from during interviews.

The First Amendment to the U.S. Constitution, Title VII of the Civil Rights Act of 1964, and various state constitutions and laws all prohibit discrimination on the basis of religion—so don't even bother with this line of questioning.

The only interview situation where religion should come up at all is when a religious organization asks about an applicant's religious affiliations for certain jobs. In general, however, you should stay away from religious issues when you're interviewing job applicants.

Of course, some applicants bring up the subject of religion themselves. If an applicant asks your company to do something to accommodate his or her religious needs, such as setting up a kosher kitchen in the employee cafeteria, explain that you aren't legally obligated to pay for such arrangements.

Political Associations

In most instances, the political, religious, and social groups that an applicant associates with or belongs to are of no concern to an employer. The lone exception is when the government asks federal job applicants to disclose this information for national security reasons.

Of course, you can ask applicants about the professional organizations they belong to and the sports and recreational activities they participate in. But keep in mind that the U.S. Constitution protects an individual's freedom of association, and don't penalize a prospective employee because he or she belongs to a group you don't approve of.

Race

In general, you shouldn't do or say anything that might give the appearance of being discriminatory, so don't ask questions regarding an applicant's race unless you need the information to gather statistics for an affirmative-action program, a state or federal grant, or some other legitimate purpose. If you have to ask for racial information, make sure the applicant volunteers it freely.

Ethnic Background

If you think you can determine an applicant's ethnic background by asking what his or her native language is, watch out! Job applicants who aren't native-born English speakers do *not* have to disclose their native language. Moreover, they'll probably interpret questions intended to identify their ethnic background as discriminatory.

You may have a legitimate interest in the languages an applicant speaks, especially if they have any bearing on the job he or she is applying for. But you should always let the applicant volunteer this information (say, on the application form) instead of asking him or her during the interview.

Residence

Employers often try to use the place where an applicant lives to pinpoint his or her social class, religion, or ethnic background, so be very careful about how you frame residence-related questions. Questions about residency are perfectly legal—but if you need this information, make sure you request it of *all* applicants. Don't appear to single out one group.

Education

If you're like most employers, you want to learn as much as possible about your prospective employees' education and training. You have every right to ask about an applicant's educational qualifications for the job at hand, as long as you're not using these questions to weed out groups protected under Title VII.

Members of minority groups often complain that employers use educational criteria as a way to shut them out of jobs for which they're otherwise qualified. Therefore, make sure the educational credentials you ask about are necessary for the job. For instance, if you're interviewing an applicant for a position as a truck driver, you can ask him or her about vocational training for learning how to drive semis but limit questions about other academic credentials.

Birthdate

Remember Richard L. from the case at the beginning of the chapter? As the nation gets older, there will be a lot more age discrimination cases like Richard's. To avoid problems in this area, don't discuss an applicant's age or birthdate unless it has something to do with the work the applicant will be performing.

Birthplace

Because some employers use place of birth as a means of discriminating against foreign or minority-group applicants, you should handle questions about an applicant's birthplace with kid gloves. "Were you born in the United States?" is acceptable, especially if licensing laws and regulations demand that the applicant be a U.S. citizen. But bypass questions about place of birth in situations where the information has no bearing on the job.

Personal Finances

An applicant's banking, borrowing, and credit practices are his or her own business. But if the applicant will handle money, precious metals, or other valuables, his or her finances (or lack of) may have some bearing on his or her qualifications for the job—or on how temptations the job presents are handled. You don't have to hire individuals with poor credit records to handle your money or valuables.

Garnishment

When an individual's salary is garnisheed, he or she must turn over an part of it to one or more creditors until a debt is paid off. Although you may frown on people who accumulate huge personal debts they can't pay back, the Federal Consumer Protection Act and similar state laws make it illegal for employers to refuse to hire an applicant who has been garnisheed.

Military Service

The United States now has an all-volunteer army, and volunteers may view military service as a part-time activity.

Some employers ask questions about military service as a way of zeroing in on prospective employees who may need to take time off to serve in the National Guard or the reserves, but you should avoid such inquiries. Something else to remember is that the Vietnam-Era Veteran's Readjustment Assistance Act prohibits discrimination against military draftees.

Don't discuss an applicant's service and discharge records unless the information is related to the job. Federal contractors sometimes have to ask applicants to submit information on their military background, especially if the job has ties to national security. But if you use military service information to cull veterans from your work force, you're asking for trouble.

Arrest History

The bedrock foundation of the American legal system is that an individual is innocent until proved guilty. This principle also applies to questions about arrests and convictions during an interview. Because most arrests do not result in conviction, many states forbid employers from delving into an applicant's arrest history unless the applicant actually was convicted.

The law makes exceptions for banks, hospitals, and other regulated industries: They can ask about an applicant's arrest history if there are security or safety issues at stake.

Name Change

You should never ask an applicant anything about names or aliases he or she may have used in the past. Members of various ethnic groups have been known to change their names to sound more "American," and asking about name changes may smack of discrimination.

Union Membership

Both the National Labor Relations Act and state laws protect membership in or affiliation with a labor union. You cannot turn down an applicant for a job because he or she is active in a union or has union connections. Of course, you have a right to ask about union membership when it affects the job, but you cannot base the hiring decision on the applicant's union affiliations.

Jury Duty

The Federal Protection of Jurors' Employment Act and similar state laws prohibit discrimination against employees who serve on juries. Judges generally look askance at employers who discriminate against an applicant who has served on a jury or who will be doing jury duty. The judicial reasoning here is very simple: Our trial-by-jury system wouldn't survive very long if employers chastised employees for serving on juries.

Photographs

If an applicant hasn't supplied a photograph with his or her résumé or application, you can't badger him or her into providing one during the interview. Actually, asking an applicant to submit a photograph with an application is now considered a form of discrimination. You shouldn't ask for a photograph unless the job requires it—for example, if the applicant is seeking a position as a security guard and a picture is necessary for identification purposes.

WHAT YOU *CAN* ASK

It may seem as if there isn't much you can ask a job applicant without getting slapped with a discrimination complaint. Actually, employers still have a lot of leeway in interviewing, as long as the interview questioning doesn't unfairly single out any specific person or group.

The at-will doctrine, though dethroned from its 19th-century eminence, governs many aspects of the employer-employee relationship today—and it gives you the right to demand the following qualities of prospective employees:

Good Attitude.   Naturally, you want employees to express a positive attitude that is in line with your company's philosophy and the image it wants to project. You have every right to expect a positive attitude from your prospective employees, too, so feel free to ask appropriate attitudinal questions.

Commitment.   You can certainly require employees to be loyal and committed to your company. This is especially true for jobs involving customer relations and product quality.

The courts have consistently upheld the right of employers to demand that applicants sign "confidentiality agreements" concerning product design, new ideas, future plans, or industry information. The courts realize that nondisclosure is vital for the survival of many businesses.

Ethical Behavior.   American employers lose billions of dollars every year to dishonest employees, and the courts support employers' efforts to prevent such losses. Therefore, you can ask a prospective employee to sign a statement saying that he or she will comply with the company's code of ethics. No one has the right to commit theft or fraud.

Proper Qualifications.   Obviously, you can't hire someone if you don't know whether he or she is able to do the job, so you have the right to ask applicants about their qualifications for a position. In addition, you can set criteria for determining who is or isn't qualified, as long as you stay within the bounds of standard industry practices and the demands of the job.

The revised at-will doctrine also acknowledges that you need to select the best-qualified person for the job by asking questions that will help you identify an applicant's skills, training, and ability to perform. Here are some guidelines:

1. You can ask an applicant to comment on his or her past work history, military service, and other job-related experience.
2. You can require an applicant to follow your company's code of ethics and personnel rules. Employers aren't expected to change the rules to fit an individual employee's needs or desires.
3. Companywide smoking bans are legal, so you can ask an applicant about his or her smoking habits. If the applicant is a smoker, you can ask him or her to abstain from smoking at work as a condition of employment.
4. You can ask an applicant to comply with rules prohibiting alcohol and drug use in the workplace as a condition of employment. The workplace is not a bar or an opium den.
5. You can ask an applicant to describe any physical problems that might prevent him or her from doing a strenuous job. If health directly affects on-the-job performance, physical condition is an appropriate criterion for employment.
6. You can inquire about an applicant's future plans or special arrangements your company may need to make if the applicant is hired, as long as the questions relate to the job.
7. You can ask questions that attempt to determine an applicant's level of maturity, state of mind, and ethical beliefs.
8. You can ask an applicant to sign a waiver authorizing you to contact references, educational institutions, former employers, and other relevant sources of preemployment information.
9. You can ask about use of aliases, previous home addresses, past and present telephone numbers, roommates, and social activities, but *only* if these things might influence on-the-job performance.
10. If your company belongs to a regulated industry such as banking or securities trading, you can ask an applicant to submit to fingerprinting and to provide his or her arrest record and court records.

INTERVIEWING TACTICS

Interviewing is an art form. Some people have an innate talent for interviewing and selecting the right applicant for the job while others struggle through the hiring process. But with a little training, most of us can improve our interviewing skills to the point where we can identify the best candidate for the job. Good, solid interviewing can reduce your risk of legal exposure, too, so try to follow these suggestions when you or your staff conduct interviews:

1. Take charge of the interview, and control the line of questioning.
2. Keep your questions short and confined to one topic at a time.
3. Ask only one question at a time, and give the interviewee plenty of time to answer.
4. Make sure your questions are clear, unambiguous, and easy to understand, especially when you're dealing with poorly educated applicants.
5. Keep a cool head, and avoid questions that might be construed as discriminatory.
6. Avoid suggestive or leading questions, which can confuse the applicant and make him or her suspicious.
7. Maintain a friendly tone. Don't be sarcastic, and never talk down to the interviewee.
8. Always be straightforward and frank in answering as well as asking questions.
9. Make sure that the applicant's answers are clear to you, and give the applicant an opportunity to qualify his or her answers.
10. Watch out for slips of the tongue and other indicators that might indicate potential personality flaws that would adversely affect job performance.

Unfortunately, people aren't always truthful or forthright, so be on the lookout for such things as:

1. Evasive and vague answers to specific questions.
2. Inconsistent answers to the same or similar questions.
3. Information that conflicts with information previously provided by the applicant.
4. Inaccurate information about former employers, dates, training, and schooling.
5. Reluctance to be specific about job experience, professional affiliations, and references.
6. Holes in the job application form or résumé that the applicant can't explain to your satisfaction during the interview.
7. Emotional reactions to questions.
8. Frequent job changes or moves that the applicant can't reasonably explain.

The interview itself should always be conducted in a relaxed setting. You want to put the applicant at ease while eliciting as much information as possible from him or her. To achieve this objective, you should:

1. Remove open files, correspondence, and other distractions from your desk.
2. Always conduct the interview in a well-lit, well-ventilated room in a businesslike setting.
3. Have someone else take your telephone calls, and turn off your radio during the interview. Close the door to minimize outside noise.
4. Have the applicant sit so that you can observe his or her body language.

Whenever you do an interview, make sure you take notes—they could prove invaluable if the applicant tries to sue you later on. In fact, you should treat your notes as if you knew they were going to be used as evidence in court: Avoid shorthand and abbreviations, write legibly in ink, and record only information pertinent to the job in question. And if you think notes aren't going to be enough and you anticipate problems, go ahead and tape the interview.

SELECTING QUALIFIED APPLICANTS

I think I can accurately assume that your hiring goal is to select the most qualified applicant who will do the best job for your company. In assessing the skills and qualifications of an applicant, you have a right to interview prospective employees about training, skills, and background that could predict or affect job performance.

Bona Fide Occupational Qualifications

As I discussed earlier in this chapter, only in rare instances can an employer ask about an applicant's age, religion, ethnicity, or medical condition. The courts and regulators make exceptions, however, if these things are "bona fide occupational qualifications" (BOQs). The BOQ exception does not give you carte blanche to pry into an applicant's personal life, but here are some examples of what it does allow:

- A company can question an applicant about his or her health and medical condition if the job requires him or her to travel extensively in Third World countries where poor medical resources and rough terrain may create legitimate health concerns.
- A church, synagogue, or temple can ask an applicant to disclose his or her religion but cannot require all its employees to hold the same religious beliefs.
- An organization that serves youth, such as a juvenile correctional facility, can ask an applicant for a position involving close contact with juveniles whether he or she has an arrest record.
- An advertising firm can ask an applicant to disclose his or her age if the job calls for someone to promote youth-directed products.
- An interviewer for an apprenticeship program can ask a candidate about his or her ethnic background if this information is needed to comply with a government-mandated quota program.

An interviewer's line of questioning could violate federal and state antidiscrimination statutes if it deals with areas that don't relate to the position in question. For instance, you can't ask an applicant for a management position whether he or she is over 50 years old because age is not a bona fide criterion for the job. Likewise, federal contractors can get into hot water under the Rehabilitation Act of 1973 if they ask engineering candidates about their health and physical condition.

Relationship to Other Workers

You can ask whether an applicant is related to other members of your work force to enforce a rule prohibiting married couples from working together. But your "no-spousal rule" must meet the following criteria:

1. It must be prompted by business needs, not by the whims of the employer. Legitimate business needs include prevention of nepotism, conflict of interest, and fraud among employees.
2. It must apply equally to both male and female job applicants, and you must make the applicant aware of the rule from the start. You're also obligated to tell the applicant the rule's specifics and the conditions under which it comes into play. It's best to give the applicant a copy of the rule in writing and to include it in your company's personnel handbook.
3. It should be flexible enough to bend to the realities of everyday life. A no-spousal rule that applies only to certain family members is more likely to survive a legal challenge than a rule with a broader scope. For instance, most courts will uphold no-spousal rules if they apply to husbands and wives working together. But if you try to extend the rule to cover sisters and nephews and cousins, the rule probably won't stand up in court.

You should be prepared to justify the existence of a no-spousal rule to an applicant at any time because the applicant may challenge your use of the rule as a reason for not hiring him or her.

You would be treading on dangerous ground if you tried to enforce a no-spousal rule under any of these circumstances:

1. The rule applies only to members of one sex, race, religion, or ethnic group.
2. The rule is actually a subtle way to enforce your personal code of morality or a bias against, say, unwed mothers or divorced men.
3. The applicant's spouse or other relations work for a competitor.
4. The applicant is married to a member of a group protected under Title VII.

Affirmative-Action Quotas

Although some employers have court-ordered hiring quotas, most do not. Unfortunately, employers who initiate voluntary affirmative-action programs risk violating Title VII, no matter how good their intentions are.

That's because Title VII also prohibits reverse discrimination, so a white male applicant who feels the interview process is offensive and discriminatory could bring a reverse-discrimination action against your company. In a good many of these cases, the EEOC has ruled in favor of employers who are trying to correct an obvious imbalance in the composition of the company's work force (see Chapter 9). But affirmative action is not a guaranteed defense against reverse-discrimination charges.

Previous Work Experience

An employer has a right to obtain detailed information about an applicant's level of experience for the position in question. Although the courts have not set guidelines regarding the type of questions you can ask an applicant to determine his or her experience, some general guidelines have emerged through precedent.

As I have repeated throughout this chapter, any questioning about an applicant's level of experience should have some connection to the job. The more complex and demanding the job, the more relevant an applicant's experience is to the potential employer.

Whenever possible, I recommend that you use standardized questions or examinations to find out about an applicant's past experience, especially for technically demanding jobs. And, of course, you should ask the same questions of all applicants, regardless of race, sex, or religion.

Education

You're not going to bump up against any privacy laws by questioning an applicant about his or her education. You have the right to inquire about an applicant's schooling and training, and to contact the high school, college, or technical training program that the applicant claims to have attended.

During the interview, you can talk about the applicant's grades and the classes he or she took, as well as his or her class rank. You can also request an explanation for any lapses in the applicant's education—for example, why he dropped out of college for two years before completing his degree.

Language

Although the Immigration Reform and Control Act of 1986 has a lot to say about how you hire foreign-born workers, it doesn't obligate you to conduct job interviews in the applicant's language or to supply an interpreter for the interview. In cases where speaking, reading, or writing English has no relevance to an applicant's ability to perform the job, however, you might consider calling in an interpreter. In areas of the United States where Spanish has become the lingua franca, you might need an interpreter for most of the applicants you see. Keep in mind, though, that if you provide an interpreter for some applicants who speak a foreign language, you must offer the interpreter's services to *all* such applicants.

Grooming and Appearance

Most disputes about dress and appearance codes eventually turn into claims of sexual and racial discrimination, so apply such codes equally to all applicants and employees. You can enforce dress or grooming codes, or ask a prospective employee about his or her appearance, in situations where grooming is directly tied to safety at the workplace—for instance, when employees with long hair handle dangerous equipment or toxic chemicals.

You can also enforce a grooming code when the applicant will have a lot of contact with the public or when the nature of the job demands a certain appearance, as in police and other paramilitary work. But be sure you don't offend an applicant whose appearance is mandated by his or her cultural or religious background.

Pregnancy and Childbearing

The bottom line is that it's illegal to discriminate against an applicant because she is pregnant or recovering from the effects of childbirth. Under the Pregnancy Discrimination Act of 1978, an amendment to the Civil Rights Act of 1964, you must treat pregnancy the same as any other disability.

Although the 1978 amendment does not specifically address issues involved in hiring, an applicant might use it to sue a prospective employer. Neither the 1978 act nor the EEOC directly concerns itself with discrimination in hiring on the basis of pregnancy, but that doesn't mean *you* shouldn't be concerned. Here are some guidelines to follow:

1. Don't give a male applicant with a disability preference over a pregnant but equally qualified female candidate.
2. Don't exclude female job applicants from consideration for employment because of pregnancy, childbirth, or a related medical condition.
3. Offer the same health insurance, disability insurance, and sick leave plans to pregnant female applicants as to male applicants. Don't deny pregnant female applicants any benefits available to their male counterparts.
4. Don't try to deny employment to a female applicant because she recently had an abortion.
5. If you're willing to make accommodations for a disabled male applicant, do the same for a pregnant female applicant.
6. Don't single out a pregnancy-related condition for special procedures.

In interviewing, you can ask about a female applicant's pregnancy or recent childbirth if it affects the job or if you'll need to make special arrangements. But you'd better be sure that the questioning *does* have something to do with the job. A good test is to compare it to the questioning you would use for a disabled male applicant; there should be no difference.

OTHER INTERVIEWING TRAPS

Although it's mainly the antidiscrimination laws that govern the way an interview is conducted, you should also be aware of other laws that can trip up an unwary employer.

Under these laws, a prospective employee can hold an employer's feet to the fire for statements the employer makes (or, for that matter, implies) during an interview, regardless of what the at-will doctrine allows.

Fraud and Deceit

It's not uncommon for a prospective employee to accept a job offer only to discover that he or she was sold a bill of goods. Using fraud or deceit to sucker an applicant into accepting a position is grounds for a lawsuit. To win such a case, the duped employee just needs to demonstrate that:

1. The employer or the employer's recruiting agency misrepresented a material fact about the job.
2. The employer knew that the offer was phony when it was made.
3. The employer made the false offer with the intention of forcing the applicant to act on it by accepting the job.
4. The applicant suffered some loss as a result of the false offer.

Defamation

In the course of the interview and other preemployment screening activities, you may come to learn many of the applicant's innermost secrets—marital situation, class rank in college, what former employers thought of him or her, and whether he or she has a criminal record. It's legal to obtain this information, and you need it to make hiring decisions. But don't forget: *It's still private information.*

Misuse or improper handling of sensitive personal information may prompt an applicant to file a defamation action. If the applicant doesn't get a job with your company, he or she is going to be less than thrilled to find out that you've leaked his or her private information to other employers without permission. Sound like a dangerous situation? You bet!

These problems frequently arise in close-knit industries or small business communities where everyone knows everyone else. If that's the kind of business environment you work in, you're going to have to take special care not to spill any beans.

There are two types of defamation: *slander* (a verbal communication or statement, possibly given over the phone by one employer to another) and *libel* (a written statement, often a letter about a potential employee). The burden of defending such actions usually falls on the employer, who must prove the truth and accuracy of the statement that he or she made, whether written or verbal.

Omissions

You don't need to tell an applicant everything about the job and environment in which he or she will be working, but you do have an obligation not to leave out anything that would affect the potential employee adversely. For instance, you should warn an applicant with a disability or medical problem about any dangerous conditions in the workplace that may impact his or her health.

If your company intends to close down the department or division for which the applicant is being considered or to shift it to another city, you must tell the applicant about these plans during the interview. The prospective employee shouldn't have to find out after he or she has accepted the job. At that point, it's too late: If the applicant opts to sue your company, he or she will probably receive a nice hunk of cash to compensate for the opportunities that he or she missed by taking the job you offered.

Error

A simple rule of thumb in interviewing is to be as specific and factual as possible. You should provide accurate information about salary, bonuses, insurance coverage, vacation time, and other work-related benefits. If you make erroneous statements, you run the risk of being held liable for falsifying job information.

Puffery

Boasting about the merits of one's products, services, or job offerings is part of the American business scene, and the practice isn't about to go away. Still, you should guard against crossing the threshold from "puffery" to outright lies. Remember: Salesmanship is acceptable; fraud is illegal.

Breach of Contract

As you know well by now, the employment relationship is a contractual one. In return for promises of job security and other benefits, an applicant agrees to accept employment. If you fail to live up to any promises that you made during an interview, you are in breach of contract. You're also out a lot of money if the applicant takes you to court.

For this reason, you should be careful when telling applicants about your company's rules, policies, and procedures, as well as any other economic benefits the applicant stands to gain from accepting a job with the company.

Emotional Distress

Sometimes an applicant alleges that a prospective employer treated him or her so badly that he or she suffered severe emotional distress as a result. To win such a claim, the applicant must show that the employer's actions were extreme, outrageous, intentional, and reckless; that it was the employer's actions that actually caused the emotional distress the applicant suffered; and that the distress was severe.

In a case of this type, an applicant sued a Maryland employer. When the applicant refused to take a polygraph examination during his interview, the employer implied that he was afraid to take the exam because he was a liar. The applicant was able to prove that the employer's actions were outrageous and led to extreme emotional distress, and he won the case.

Assault and Battery

Allegations of assault and battery most commonly come up in sexual harassment cases—for example, a female applicant claims that an interviewer made sexual advances to her or touched her in a "sexually explicit manner."

If you suspect that you're dealing with a potentially unstable female applicant, you would be wise to call in a second interviewer. Also, be guarded in your mannerisms and demeanor during the interview. Most courts are reluctant to believe sexual assault and battery charges without additional evidence, but some have proved willing to do so if the interviewer has a history of similar behavior.

The interview is an extremely crucial step in selecting the best person for the job. But it is also fraught with potentially dangerous situations for employers. My best advice is:

Confine the interview to inquiries and questions that directly relate to the job.

Apply your standards equally to all applicants, regardless of race, sex, religion, or ethnic background.

CHAPTER 7

THE FEDERAL REGULATORS

Laws wouldn't be worth the paper they're written on without some way to enforce them—and employment laws are no exception.

You might think the people who enforce our employment laws are the judges who hear cases between applicants and potential employers, or perhaps the litigants who figure that charges of hiring discrimination and other employment-related problems are worth taking to court. But the real "gunslingers" in employment law enforcement are the federal and local regulators—the agencies that make the rules in the first place.

At the federal level, the Department of Labor bears most of the brunt for ensuring that the hiring practices of American employers meet the law's requirements. Under the Labor Department's umbrella, the principal enforcement agencies are the Equal Employment Opportunity Commission (EEOC) and the Office of Federal Contract Compliance Programs (OFCCP).

At the local level are state attorney generals, human rights commissions, and a potpourri of county and city antidiscrimination agencies. In fact, more than 40 states now have mini-EEOC agencies which are modeled after their federal counterpart and work closely with it to enforce antidiscrimination laws.

Employers who run afoul of the regulatory agencies should be prepared to open their pocketbooks very wide, as these cases show:

• A federal judge in Chicago ruled that one of the nation's largest telecommunications companies discriminated against pregnant employees by forcing them to take early maternity leave, reducing their likelihood of being reinstated in the jobs they held before and limiting their seniority rights. The judge made this ruling in a class action suit filed by the EEOC. The matter hasn't been resolved yet, but when it finally is, the telecommunications company may be out more than $10 million.

• Thousands of former and current minority employees of an Illinois bank shared $14 million in back pay in the largest settlement ever of a federal discrimination case against a single employer. The U.S. Department of Labor had sued on behalf of the employees under Executive Order 11246, alleging that the minority workers had been paid less than white workers with similar backgrounds.

But big-money lawsuits are just the tip of the iceberg. The rules the regulators make affect the hiring decisions you make every day, so you'd better pay attention to them.

Take the recent EEOC directive that prohibits employers from refusing to hire female job applicants on the grounds that exposing women to on-the-job chemicals or radioactivity could impair their ability to bear children, or damage children they might already be carrying. It's estimated that some 20 million jobs in the United States expose workers (both male and female) to possible reproductive harm, so the EEOC directive is bound to influence a lot of hiring decisions in the future.

EEOC sources report that this directive was prompted by concern that employers might exaggerate the risks of jobs involving hazardous chemicals or radiation as a means of shutting out female job applicants. Of course, the materials used at some workplaces *are* extremely dangerous to human beings. But if such materials really do pose a threat of reproductive damage or put fetuses at risk at a work site, the employer has to give the EEOC concrete scientific evidence to support his or her decision not to hire women.

Employers who attract attention from the federal regulators soon wish that they hadn't. The ensuing investigations and court cases are not only expensive but time-consuming: In one instance, the OFCCP ordered a company to produce every one of its payroll records for a 15-year period.

But outright violations of the law aren't the only thing that draw fire from the regulators. As often as not, it's ignorance of the regulatory process that gets employers in trouble. To avoid hassles with the regulators, you need to know how the regulatory maze governs your day-to-day employment practices and how the most important regulators operate.

WHAT DO THE REGULATORS DO?

Both the federal and local regulators play a bigger role in our lives than most of us can possibly imagine. They influence the daily decision-making process of government at all levels, as well as the social and economic dealings of almost every segment of our society. Regulatory agencies have a say in how employers and employees interact with each other, how companies and government agencies select and train their employees, and how everyone hires and fires.

Although each regulatory agency has a very different structure and jurisdiction, most of them share the following characteristics:

Types of Regulation
In a traditional regulatory scheme, an agency oversees specific, identifiable industries. An example is the OFCCP's jurisdiction over federal contractors and their subcontractors. But there is also a new regulatory wave that cuts across industry lines. The EEOC, for instance, has jurisdiction over *all* public and private employers with 15 or more agencies. The big difference is that traditional regulation focuses on the government while new regulation is more universal—it's not directed at any single business or employment problem.

Mandate
The legal basis for federal regulation lies in the U.S. Constitution's Commerce Clause, which gives Congress the power to "regulate commerce with foreign nations and among the several

states." Congress establishes the regulatory agencies and gives them broad mandates to control the daily activities of the private sector. Whether at the federal or the local level, the regulators have the power both to prescribe and enforce rules and regulations. A regulatory body acts as an all-in-one investigator, prosecutor, and judge.

Rule-Making Process

At all levels, regulatory agencies also act as legislative bodies, issuing and interpreting rules and regulations. Before an agency can issue a new rule, however, it must ask the public and, of course, the industry it regulates. Both the public and members of the regulated industry get a chance to offer written or verbal comments on the agency's proposed rule. If there are any objections to the rule, the person or business making the objection must let the agency know *before* the rule is adopted.

Regulatory agencies can repeal or amend their existing rules, too. If a federal regulatory agency wants to change one of its rules, it must start by publishing its intentions in the *Federal Register*. State and local regulators run similar notices in appropriate government organs or newspapers.

Wherever it's published, the notice announces the proposed rule change and invites the public to comment on it. Any interested member of the public can submit written or oral testimony. Once the agency has decided to make the change, it must publish the proposed or modified rule before adopting it. Then there's one last round of soliciting comments and inviting members of the public to offer additional testimony.

Interpretations

The regulatory agencies have the power to issue new or modified interpretations of their old employment regulations—rules that clarify discrepancies for agency staffs as well as employers. An agency's interpretations can take several forms, including press releases, formal rulings, and rulings by one of the agency's administrative law judges.

The thing to remember about interpretations by regulatory agencies is that they're not always binding; you can challenge them in court. The court is the final arbitrator, and judges have been known to disagree with regulatory agencies. In most cases, however, a court will probably not rush to overturn a regulatory decision.

Compliance

The federal and local regulators can use several legal vehicles to encourage employers to comply with their rules. They can invoke their powers to enact environmental and safety guidelines, to investigate and prosecute complaints, and to develop hiring guidelines for companies in industries such as aviation, banking, and nuclear energy. They can even demand financial disclosures from employers or amplify applicant and employee privacy rights.

Investigations

All regulatory agencies have the authority to conduct formal and informal investigations. Many of these probes result in administrative or civil actions; a handful lead to criminal prosecutions. The EEOC can refer violations of its consent decrees to the U.S. Department of Justice for criminal prosecution as well as civil action. (When the EEOC negotiates a consent decree to settle a claim of employment discrimination, the employer agrees not to discriminate in the future without admitting that he or she actually did anything wrong in the past.)

But the regulators don't have unbridled investigative powers, thanks to various constitutional and statutory restrictions. Basically, one hand gives while the other takes away: Although the courts have awarded the regulatory agencies broad rule-making powers, they've fenced in the regulators' investigative domain.

The OFCCP, for example, can launch an investigation whenever it suspects discrimination in hiring by a federal contractor; however, the office doesn't have the authority to investigate similar infractions in the private sector. That's because private businesses fall outside the OFCCP's jurisdiction.

The regulators can issue subpoenas, visit work sites, and meet with an employer's representatives. But many courts require a regulatory agency to have a reasonable basis to believe that there's been a violation of the law before doing any of these things. In some situations, the courts may even demand that the regulator obtain a search warrant before seizing an employer's business records. Still, the regulatory agency has the right to go to court to enforce administrative subpoenas that it issues for records and other evidence.

Hearings

The investigations that regulatory agencies conduct sometimes end up as administrative hearings. An administrative hearing is a quasi-judicial proceeding that's much like a trial. Regulatory agencies use administrative hearings to resolve disputed factual questions or to determine whether an employer has violated any of the agency's rules and regulations.

The agency's administrative law judge oversees the hearing. During the proceedings, the agency's staff and the employer's attorney get equal time to present testimony and evidence, and to cross-examine each other's witnesses. At the conclusion of the hearing, the judge hands down a decision. If the employer isn't happy with that decision, he or she can appeal to the head of the agency or turn to the courts.

The testimony and evidence presented at these hearings are usually open to the public. In fact, the hearings themselves often serve as informal "discovery vehicles" for plaintiffs: The testimony and evidence introduced at an administrative hearing can be used in a civil suit. Occasionally, however, a hearing may be closed. If that happens, you can call on the Freedom of Information Act, as described in Chapter 1, to gain access to the evidence presented at the hearing.

THE "FEDS"

A Syracuse University analysis of 280 federal court cases involving claims under the Age Discrimination in Employment Act found that managers and professionals were responsible for more than half of the suits. The analysis also revealed that white men filed 84 percent of the claims.

The results of this study dispel the notion, common among employers, that *only* women and members of minority groups turn to the regulators and the courts if they want legal relief from discrimination. In fact, only the savviest and most sophisticated members of the American work force really understand how to use the federal regulatory system to their advantage. (Of course, those with regulatory know-how also tend to have the financial backing to pursue their grievances with the federal agencies.)

You never know when one of these savvy individuals is going to apply for a job at your company, so it pays to develop a few regulatory smarts of your own.

At the federal level, employment regulation rests with the Departments of Labor and Justice. The Department of Labor and its agencies are responsible for the lion's share of employment regulation. But the Immigration Reform and Control Act of 1986 will certainly mean a meatier role for the Justice Department in the future.

Department of Labor

Created in 1884 as the Bureau of Labor, the Department of Labor sees its charter as fostering, promoting, and improving the welfare of America's workers. That implies bettering their working conditions and giving all workers equal access to opportunities in the workplace.

To carry out this vital task, the department administers more than 130 federal laws dealing with some aspect of the employer-employee relationship. The department has the authority to police these areas:

1. Hiring and firing practices.
2. Job applicant and employee testing.
3. Preemployment screening and background checks.
4. Applicant interviews.
5. Affirmative action.
6. Antidiscrimination laws.
7. Job advertisements.

In other words, just about everything covered in this book falls under the aegis of the Department of Labor.

The department's decision making rests with several key officials. The best-known is the secretary of labor, who heads the department. As a member of the cabinet, the secretary serves as the president's principal adviser on labor matters. Traditionally, someone with close ties to labor or management has held the post, but this is certainly not a hard-and-fast rule.

The solicitor heads the department's legal staff and is its legal adviser. The solicitor's office coordinates and litigates many of the prosecutions filed by the department under these laws:

1. Occupational Safety and Health Act.
2. Employee Retirement Security Act.
3. Fair Labor Standards Act.
4. Longshoremen's and Labor Workers' Compensation Act.
5. Farm Labor Contractor Registration Act.

The solicitor's staff also represents the department in its administrative hearings and handles its appeals. The Department of Justice, however, is in charge of criminal prosecutions, and the Labor Department's field offices take care of regional cases.

The inspector general handles the Labor Department's in-house investigations. The inspector general's staff also audits and investigates allegations of fraud, theft, and waste in the department's programs, especially if they involve labor union pension or welfare funds, or unauthorized actions by department personnel.

Of course, these three officials can't enforce the labor laws all by themselves. They get help with the department's day-to-day operations from more than a dozen bureaus, divisions, and semiautonomous agencies. Here are the major players:

Office of Administrative Law Judges

The judges preside over formal hearings to determine violations of minimum wage requirements, overtime payments, compensation benefits, discrimination in hiring or firing, alien certification, employee protection, and health and safety regulations. The laws that give them their authority to pass judgment on such issues include:

1. Longshoremen's and Harbor Workers' Compensation Act.
2. Contract Workers and Safety Standards Act.
3. Davis–Bacon Act.
4. Occupational Safety and Health Act.

5. Fair Labor Standards Act.
6. Black Lung Benefits Act.
7. Immigration and Nationality Act.
8. Toxic Substance Control Act.
9. Clean Air Act.
10. Energy Reorganization Act.
11. Various executive orders.

Office of Federal Contract Compliance Programs

The OFCCP's main job is to establish antidiscrimination policies and goals for achieving equality in employment by federal contractors and in federally assisted construction programs. It's also responsible for ensuring that government contractors and subcontractors do their best to hire Vietnam veterans and applicants with physical disabilities, and to give these employees opportunities to advance through company ranks.

The OFCCP works with the EEOC and the Department of Justice to enforce Title VII of the Civil Rights Act of 1964, and acts as a liaison with other agencies that deal with civil rights and equal employment opportunity.

Recall from Chapter 1, the OFCCP handles all discrimination complaints under Executive Order 11246. An applicant or employee would file such a complaint if he or she felt a federal contractor or subcontractor had discriminated in hiring or firing on the basis of race, color, religion, sex, national origin, or physical disability.

An applicant can file a complaint by phone or letter, or can drop in to the OFCCP's Washington, D.C., office or one of its regional branches. Individuals or organizations can also file complaints on behalf of those affected by discrimination. Complaints must be filed within 180 days of the discriminatory act; the OFCCP won't extend the deadline unless the applicant or employee has a good reason for filing late. The complaint should include a description of the discriminatory act, the names and addresses of the federal contractor and of individuals who allegedly were discriminated against, and any other information that might help the investigation.

After receiving a complaint, the OFCCP may decide to

launch an investigation straightaway. If the complaint involves discrimination against only one person, however, the OFCCP may opt to pass it on to the EEOC instead. The OFCCP tends to focus its concern on discriminatory hiring and firing practices that affect good-sized segments of an employer's work force, rather than just one worker.

If an OFCCP investigation indicates that a federal contractor or subcontractor has violated Executive Order 11246, the office tries to negotiate a conciliation agreement. Under such an agreement, the contractor might have to hire a job applicant or give an employee a promotion. If an employer is stubborn about not signing a conciliation agreement, the OFCCP can initiate an administrative process that includes a formal hearing.

But government contractors seldom gain anything by thumbing their noses at the OFCCP. Contractors who don't comply with Executive Order 11246 can lose their current contracts or be barred from future federal contract work. The government can withhold payment for work already done. And, to truly rub salt in the wound, the Department of Justice can sue the contractor in federal court on behalf of the Department of Labor.

Occupational Safety and Health Administration
The assistant secretary for occupational safety and health heads OSHA, an agency established by the Occupational Safety and Health Act of 1970.

This act applies to just about every employer in the country. Enforced (as you might expect) by the Department of Labor, the act requires employers to make sure the workplace where their employees must spend their days does not contain hazards that might physically harm or even kill them. The act's protection extends to applicants who accept a job with a company as well as to current employees.

OSHA develops occupational safety and health standards, issues regulations, and carries out investigations and inspections to ensure that employers comply with its safety and health guidelines. If an employer violates OSHA regulations, an OSHA inspector can issue a citation and suggest penalties. The agency has offices in 10 regions throughout the United States.

Occupational Safety and Health Review Commission

Also established by the Occupational Safety and Health Act of 1970, the three-member Occupational Safety and Health Review Commission (OSHRC) is an independent, quasi-judicial agency that rules on cases forwarded to it by the Department of Labor. Usually, these cases involve disagreements over the findings of OSHA inspections.

Employers have the right to dispute alleged job safety or health violations revealed during an OSHA inspection, as well as the penalties OSHA proposes and the time frame OSHA gives the employer for correcting hazardous situations. Employees and their representatives can initiate a case by challenging the amount of time OSHA has allowed an employer to do something about a condition that violates the Occupational Safety and Health Act.

OSHRC may have a case to decide if an employer, employee, or representative contests an OSHA citation within 15 working days after the inspector issued it. A case that requires a hearing is assigned to one of OSHRC's administrative law judges. Ordinarily, the hearing is held in the community where the alleged violation occurred or as close to that community as possible. At the hearing, OSHRC has the burden of proving the case.

Most of the decisions issued by OSHRC administrative law judges become final, but each decision is also subject to discretionary review by OSHRC itself. Any of the three members of the commission can question a decision, but the review must take place within 30 days after the decision was filed. When this happens, the commission issues its own decision. That's not always the end of the story, however: Even after OSHRC has ruled on a case, an employer or employee who has been adversely affected by the decision can carry the case to the U.S. Court of Appeals.

Women's Bureau

This agency is responsible for formulating standards and policies to improve working conditions for female employees in the United States. It also investigates and reports to the Department of Labor on the working conditions of women in industry.

Labor–Management Service Administration

The assistant secretary for labor–management relations is the chief administrator of the Labor–Management Service Administration (LMSA).

This agency aids veterans and members of the reserves and the National Guard in claiming their employment rights. For instance, if a male worker joins the National Guard and has to go on active duty for a few weeks every summer, his employer can't penalize him by giving his job to someone else, closing him off from accrued seniority benefits and higher-status positions, or cutting his wages. If the LMSA isn't successful in achieving employment rights for a returning veteran or reservist, it can refer the case to the Department of Justice for action.

Equal Employment Opportunity Commission

Although the EEOC belongs to the Department of Labor, it's the most visible arm of the department and is really in a class by itself. The EEOC participates in the development of employment antidiscrimination laws by issuing guidelines, publishing its most important decisions, and getting involved in litigation where necessary. If you're going to brush up against any of the federal regulators, it will probably be the EEOC—all the more reason to understand how this powerful agency does what it does.

Created by Title VII of the Civil Rights Act of 1964, the EEOC has been up and running since July 2, 1965. The agency is responsible for enforcing Title VII and subsequent amendments to the Civil Rights Act of 1964 that forbid, among other things, discrimination in employment on the basis of race, color, religion, sex, or national origin. Since 1979, the EEOC has also enforced the Age Discrimination in Employment Act of 1967, which protects workers 40 years of age and older, and the Federal Equal Pay Act of 1963, which protects all workers against sex-based discrimination in pay.

In the federal sector, the EEOC's bailiwick includes affirmative-action planning, hearings, and appeals. The EEOC supervises the processing of equal-employment-opportunity complaints filed under Title VII, the Age Discrimination in Employment Act, the Equal Pay Act, and section 501 of the Rehabilitation Act of

1973. To top it all off, the EEOC administers Executive Order 12067, which oversees and coordinates all federal regulations, practices, and policies having to do with equal employment opportunity.

Through its 49 field offices, the EEOC can hear complaints of discrimination against both public and private employers. Here's how some of these complaints work:

Title VII Complaints

Applicants and employees can charge employers in private industry or in state or local government with Title VII violations, but they must file their charges with the EEOC within 180 days of the alleged violation (the deadline is extended to 300 days if the applicant or employee initially contacted a state or local fair employment practices agency). The EEOC must notify the employer within 10 days of receiving a new charge of discrimination.

Before the EEOC investigates any Title VII charges, local fair employment practices agencies must take a look at them first. Of course, this "deferral condition" applies only to states and cities that have a fair employment practices law and an agency to enforce it. The deferral period is 120 days for an agency that has been operating less than one year. Under a work-sharing agreement between the local agencies and the EEOC, however, the EEOC routinely takes jurisdiction over certain discrimination charges and starts investigating them immediately instead of waiting for the deferral period to expire.

Under Title VII, the EEOC has instituted procedural regulations that encourage disputants to settle discrimination charges "out of court"—before the EEOC evaluates the merits of the charges. The EEOC may also require fact-finding conferences as part of its investigation and as a way to build a framework for a negotiated settlement.

If an EEOC investigation finds there's reasonable cause to believe that discrimination occurred, the district or area EEOC office tries to correct the alleged illegal practices through informal methods—conciliation, conference, and persuasion.

Human beings are not always reasonable creatures, though, and conciliatory moves may fall flat. If the EEOC can't obtain an acceptable conciliation agreement between the employer and the complainant, it can sue the employer in federal district court 30 days after the date the charge was first filed. The attorney general handles the suit when charges involve a state or local government, federal agency, or political subdivision.

If the EEOC or the attorney general doesn't follow through by bringing a suit when the investigation ends (or earlier, if the person making the charges requests it), a "notice of right-to-sue" is issued that lets the party making the charges proceed to federal court within 90 days. In some instances, the EEOC may step back in if it feels a case is of interest to the public.

Age Discrimination Complaints

Applicants and employees must file age discrimination charges with the EEOC within 180 days of the alleged violation. As with Title VII violations, the filing deadline is extended to 300 days if a state has a law prohibiting age discrimination and a means of enforcing it.

The person making the charges can file a lawsuit after waiting 60 days for the EEOC to attempt to use conciliation, conference, and persuasion to get the company to stop being "ageist" in its hiring practices. If the EEOC eventually decides to take the complainant's charges to court, the name of the individual who first made the age discrimination charges will be kept confidential. The complainant can initiate a private suit in federal court, but only if the EEOC chooses not to sue on his or her behalf.

Equal Pay Complaints

Either the EEOC or a complainant can file a suit under the Equal Pay Act of 1967; there are no prerequisites for filing individual suits under this law. As with suits under the Age Discrimination Act, the name of the person filing the complaint is kept confidential. Employees can recover back wages for up to two years before the suit is filed. In cases of willful violation by the employer, employees can sue for up to three years of back pay.

Complaints against Government Employers

Federal employees or applicants who want to file complaints of job discrimination because of race, color, national origin, sex, religion, age, or physical or mental disability must start by consulting their agency's equal-employment-opportunity counselor within 30 days of the alleged act. If the complaint cannot be resolved through informal negotiations, the EEOC can file a formal complaint within 15 days after the final interview with the counselor.

A federal employee can file a complaint against a government agency or department under the Age Discrimination in Employment Act of 1967. The employee must file his or her complaint with the agency or department head, director of equal employment opportunity, head of the field installation, equal-employment-opportunity officer, federal women's program manager, or the Hispanic employment program manager.

A federal worker who wants to file a complaint under the Equal Pay Act of 1967 doesn't need to follow any of these procedures. He or she can file the complaint directly with the EEOC within two years of the alleged violation, with assurances that it will remain confidential. This act also lets employees go straight to court without having to deal with the agencies they work for or even the EEOC.

Department of Justice

As pointed out earlier, America's two employment law "cops" are the departments of Labor and Justice. You might think that the Department of Justice merely picks up the ball when a case moves into criminal territory or otherwise gets too hot for the Department of Labor to handle, but that's not so. The Justice Department has more to do with employment law enforcement than you might think.

Established in 1870 with the attorney general as its head, the U.S. Department of Justice has been aptly called the "people's law firm." Like the Department of Labor, it consists of more than a dozen bureaus and semiautonomous agencies. As far as hiring practices go, these are the agencies of the department that you should know about:

Civil Rights Division

Directed by an assistant attorney general, this division is responsible for enforcing federal civil rights laws that prohibit discrimination on the basis of race, national origin, religion, and, in some instances, sex, age, or disability. The laws that give the division its authority include the Civil Rights Acts of 1957, 1964, and 1968; the Equal Credit Opportunity Act (as amended in 1976); and the Civil Rights of Institutionalized Persons Act of 1980.

In addition, the division is in charge of implementing Executive Order 12250, adopted November 2, 1980. This order mandates coordination of efforts by executive agencies and departments to eliminate discrimination based on race, color, national origin, sex, religion, and disability in programs receiving federal financial aid, and discrimination based on disability in programs conducted by the federal government.

As mentioned, the division handles some of the civil rights actions brought by the Department of Labor and the EEOC. It also has the authority to conduct its own investigations, which are independent of those carried out by the EEOC and other Department of Labor agencies.

Immigration and Naturalization Service

The INS is one of the Justice Department's most famous (or infamous, depending on which side of the border you're on) branches. It's responsible for enforcing the nation's immigration laws, including the Immigration Reform and Control Act (IRCA) of 1986.

The service must ensure that employers comply with IRCA and hire only authorized workers. INS agents can visit work sites and ask employers to produce their hiring records. An employer who doesn't do what an INS agent requests is begging for both civil and criminal sanctions.

Under immigration law, only U.S. citizens, permanent resident aliens, and people with the following special visas can work in the United States:

1. A, G, and NATO visas for individuals employed by foreign governments, international organizations, and quasi-government agencies.
2. B-1, E-1, E-2, and I visas for employees of foreign companies working in the United States.
3. J, F, and M visas for students who have been given permission to work.

4. L, E-1, and E-2 visas for employees of firms with corporate subsidiaries doing business in the United States.
5. E-2 and L-1 visas for individuals who have invested in U.S. companies.
6. H-1, H-2, H-3, L-1, N, E-1, and E-2 visas for foreign workers employed by American companies in the United States.
7. H-1 and H-2 visas for performers working in the U.S. entertainment industry.

What you need to watch out for are applicants holding B-2, C, and D visas. Individuals with these visas are *not* authorized to work in the United States.

WHERE TO GET REGULATORY INFORMATION

You don't have to go to your company attorney to learn about federal regulatory developments that might affect your hiring practices. In fact, you'll probably find much of the information you need in these public sources:

1. *United States Statutes at Large* contain all federal statutes, joint and concurrent resolutions of Congress, presidential proclamations, reorganization plans, and constitutional amendments.
2. *United States Reports* contain all decisions and orders of the U.S. Supreme Court. The reports provide the full texts of all signed opinions, a record of orders granting or denying petitions, the court's rulings on its obligation to accept appeals cases for review, and opinions of individual Supreme Court justices in chambers.
3. *United States Supreme Court Records and Briefs* contains all legal briefs and other official materials relating to cases brought before the U.S. Supreme Court.
4. *Index to Code of Federal Regulations* includes cross-referenced subject headings, plus supplementary lists of descriptive and reserved code of federal regulations headings. It's published annually.

5. The *Congressional Record* contains official transcripts of debates and other floor proceedings of Congress, including the texts of bills. Along with the well-known daily editions, there is an annual edition of the *Record*.

You can order these publications from the superintendent of documents in Washington, D.C., or from the public information officers of the various regulatory agencies.

Of course, it's not always easy to understand the "legalese" in government sources; you may have to call in the company attorney to translate from time to time. But it's worth the trouble, I think, to keep up with what the regulators are doing. Remember:

**Federal and local regulations affect
almost all of your employment activities.**

Play by the rules and regulations, and you should be all right.

CHAPTER 8

HOW TO FEND OFF
DISCRIMINATION CHARGES

Hiring can sometimes be a no-win proposition for employers. In your ongoing quest to find the best person for the job, you advertise for candidates with a certain level of educational attainment, and you give a few tests to all the applicants who respond. Just when you have the perfect prospect (who just happens to be white and male) in the bag, a less-than-perfect candidate (who just happens to be black and female) slaps a lawsuit on your company for discriminatory hiring practices.

The spectre of discrimination charges looms behind every job application these days. The following cases demonstrate just how careful you have to be:

• The interviewer for a trucking company's personnel department asked a would-be driver if he'd ever used drugs. The applicant responded honestly that he'd used drugs in college but didn't use them any more. As the interview wrapped up, the applicant asked about his prospects for getting the job. "Everything looks good," the interviewer replied.

Two weeks later, however, the applicant learned that the trucking company had offered the job to someone else. Apparently, the company was afraid that hiring the applicant might violate U.S. Department of Transportation regulations on drugs in the workplace. The applicant sued the trucking company for discrimination in hiring.

• A young woman applied for a position with a large jewelry firm. While she was filling out her application, the personnel manager asked her if she had ever been arrested. She noted that she'd been arrested once for driving while intoxicated, but the charges had been dropped.

The personnel manager then asked the applicant to agree to a credit check. "You'll be handling very valuable merchandise," he said, "and we want to be sure that it doesn't walk away." The valuables didn't walk out of the store, but the applicant did—right to the local human rights commission where she filed charges of discrimination.

• A company had a long history of discriminating against female employees. In fact, the EEOC had cited it several times for discriminatory hiring practices. Under new management, however, the company tried to make amends for its past wrongs by voluntarily setting hiring quotas for female workers. A few months after this system was implemented, a male applicant who had been turned down for a job filed a reverse-discrimination complaint with the local counterpart of the EEOC.

Discrimination is a catch-22. Even if discriminating against groups protected under Title VII is the farthest thing from your mind, the courts may still say that you've done something discriminatory. For that matter, noble intentions don't exonerate an employer from discrimination charges.

Of course, employers sometimes use unfair tactics to shut women and members of minority groups out of jobs. But the courts have done a good job of squelching such practices.

Under the "discriminatory impact" principle, for instance, the courts have prohibited hiring practices such as word-of-mouth recruiting by mostly white employees, seniority preemployment inquiries relating to arrest records, and highly discretionary and subjective hiring decisions by white personnel managers.

The courts have also evolved the "sex plus" principle, which strikes down employment qualifications related solely to sex. Thus, an airline can't require its female flight attendants to be unmarried, nor can it refuse to hire unwed mothers.

But the courts aren't unreasonable: They recognize that employers may have legitimate reasons not to hire certain individuals or groups. Hiring right means hiring the best applicants without ruffling any discriminatory feathers in the process. And it's not really that hard to do.

A STRONG DEFENSE

Over the years, both the courts and the regulators have come to realize that there are times when employers need more latitude in hiring than the law gives them. In other words, it's not always discriminatory to turn down certain persons or groups of people. The law certainly doesn't demand that you hire everyone who walks through your door!

Understanding the exceptions to the antidiscrimination rules is the key to defending yourself against discrimination charges if the need ever arises. Even if you wield one of these defenses successfully, however, the courts are likely to be very picky about which workers you can legally bar from your workplace.

Business Necessity

The U.S. Supreme Court has acknowledged that employers can implement hiring practices that exclude members of a particular group from employment as long as the motives for excluding these applicants are purely job related. By extension, an exclusionary hiring policy or practice is acceptable if you can show that it's essential to your company's safe, efficient operation.

The courts have applied this "business necessity exception" to allow employers not to hire applicants who might:

1. Be extremely dangerous to co-workers or the public.
2. Cause serious economic disruptions to the employer's business.
3. Place the employer at severe disadvantage.
4. Cause serious breaches in workplace health and safety.
5. Pose a threat to the health and safety of the employer's customers.

Business necessity is also the legal vehicle that gives you the right not to hire applicants who don't have the required physical attributes or dexterity to do a particular job.

But business necessity is not synonymous with business *convenience*. Neither the EEOC nor the courts will accept these rationalizations:

1. Not hiring certain groups of workers would make it easier for the company to do its business.
2. Hiring certain groups would damage the company's image or reputation.
3. Clients and others who deal with the company might object if certain groups of workers were hired.
4. The company would incur additional costs to accommodate the prospective employees.
5. Hiring certain groups of workers would offend foreign businesses or governments and undermine the employer's competitive position in their markets.

If you want to use the business necessity exception, you must be prepared to show that it would be impractical to hire members of a certain group and that such a hiring policy is absolutely imperative for your company's successful operation.

Laws such as the Age Discrimination in Employment Act explicitly recognize the defense of business necessity to justify employment practices that might otherwise seem unfair. Of course, if you do refuse to hire older employees you'd better have a good business-related reason. Age has to affect the function of your business in a big way—you can't use it as a subterfuge for getting around the law.

Title VII also allows for a business necessity exception: You can refuse to hire members of certain groups if the "normal operation" of your business demands it. But it's up to you to show *why* such practices are so vital to normal business operations.

Both Title VII and the Age Discrimination in Employment Act permit the business necessity exception if it's already a part of federal or state law. Examples include compulsory retirement laws and age ceilings for commercial airline pilots.

Bona Fide Occupational Qualification

Though related to the business necessity exception, the bona fide occupational qualification (BOQ) is a more limited defense. It comes from section 703(e) of Title VII which says that an employer *can* discriminate on the basis of religion, sex, or national origin to ensure the normal operations of a business or enterprise.

The EEOC guidelines define the BOQ exception in rather narrow terms. It doesn't apply at all to racial discrimination. Actually, it's rarely invoked as a defense against charges of discrimination based on religion or national origin. Where it crops up primarily is in sex-discrimination cases.

The courts have recognized the validity of the BOQ exception under these circumstances:

1. When the employee's sex is necessary to impart authenticity or genuineness to the job (e.g., fashion models).
2. When not all applicants can perform the same job (e.g., some sports teams).
3. When the job absolutely demands members of one sex or the other (e.g., restroom attendants).

But the courts will not uphold a BOQ defense if the employer:

1. Uses it primarily to justify requiring employees to weigh at least 160 pounds.
2. Argues that members of one sex have more dexterity than members of the other sex.
3. Takes for granted that women are "weaker" and less mechanically inclined than men.
4. Assumes that the turnover rate for female workers is higher than for their male counterparts because of marriage and childbearing.
5. Claims that women cannot be aggressive salespersons or handle demanding jobs.
6. States that the company's co-workers, customers, or clients prefer male to female employees.
7. Argues that the company would have to construct separate facilities for men and women (unless the expenses for doing this would be outrageous).

Usually, the courts view BOQ defenses with suspicion. The test they use is whether "all or substantially all" women have the ability to do the job in question. If the majority of female applicants cannot do a particular job for your company, you can probably invoke the BOQ exception.

Compliance with State Laws

Many states have enacted laws and administrative regulations on hiring women, and some of them run counter to federal requirements.

For instance, numerous state laws prohibit or limit the employment of women under certain circumstances. Employers don't have to hire women for jobs requiring strenuous physical labor or exposure to dangerous chemicals, or jobs that entail working for more than a specified number of hours or for a certain period before or after childbirth. As hard as it may be to believe in these days of liberated women, such restrictions are perfectly legal under the "female-protective" laws of many states.

The only thing wrong with this picture is that female-protective laws are discriminatory and generally don't stand up in federal court or EEOC hearings. Interestingly, though, an employer who uses such laws as a defense against Title VII violations will probably not suffer too harshly in court. Judges have been reluctant to impose damages on employers who have obviously complied in good faith with state laws even though the state statutes technically violate federal antidiscrimination laws. Why penalize people who think they're following the law?

It's a tough balancing act, but you should try to comply with both federal and state laws. If you're clever, you can make it work. For instance, if the law in your state calls for special rest periods for female employees, give your male employees the same rest periods. Remember: It's up to you to demonstrate that you've complied *in good faith* with the state law. And you can't use the state law as an excuse for not complying with the federal law.

EEOC Opinions

You might be able to avoid a federal investigation if you can show that you acted (or failed to act) in good faith because you relied on EEOC opinions or written interpretations of the antidiscrimination laws. This holds true even if the courts or the EEOC eventually modifies or overturns these opinions.

Bear in mind, however, that the only things that qualify legally as "written opinions and interpretations" are "Opinion Letter" documents signed by the EEOC's general counsel and opinions published in the *Federal Register*.

U.S. Supreme Court rulings are, of course, the law of the land, so it goes without saying that they supersede EEOC opinions. If the Supreme Court, or even a high appellate court, says that you can refuse to hire certain groups of workers, the EEOC can't do much about it.

For instance, the Supreme Court has upheld the legitimacy of drug and alcohol testing for some groups of prospective employees in the transportation industry. Drug and alcohol tests, as we've seen, violate the laws of several states and can seem discriminatory. But don't worry about such infractions if you want to test engine drivers or supertanker crew members—you have a Supreme Court ruling to back you up.

Statute of Limitations

The Rehabilitation Act of 1973 and Title VII both require complainants to file charges within 180 days of the alleged act of discrimination. Prospective employees who wait too long to file may not have a case because you can successfully use the statute of limitations to deflect their discrimination complaints or suits. The courts often dismiss employment-related suits because complainants miss their filing deadlines.

Filing Flaws

Both federal and state antidiscrimination laws require complainants to go before state human rights commissions, the EEOC, and other administrative bodies before taking their complaints to court. Court is a last-ditch effort, especially in discrimination cases involving race, sex, religion, or national origin. If a complainant tries to bypass this process by going directly to the courts, you can ask the judge to dismiss the case for failure to exhaust administrative remedies first.

In breach-of-contract cases and other wrongful discharge suits, however, a complainant *can* go directly to court without having to wade through the administrative channels. The regulators may be able to enforce their own rules, but they have no enforcement powers when it comes to things like wrongful discharge.

You can also argue that the complainant has not filed with the appropriate agency. An applicant can't file an immigration-related discrimination complaint with the EEOC, for instance, because the Immigration and Naturalization Service has jurisdiction over such complaints under the Immigration Reform and Control Act of 1986. If a prospective employee files a complaint with the wrong agency, you can move to dismiss it on the grounds of "lack of jurisdiction." The same goes for suits filed with the wrong court—if a complainant files in, say, federal rather than state court.

AN ACTIVE OFFENSE

If you take action on your own to remedy past abuses in hiring, you stand a good chance of not having to pay damages if a judge imposes them in a discrimination suit. A good-faith effort to make amends for previous wrongs isn't as solid or complete a defense as some of the others I've discussed in this chapter. Still, the courts and the EEOC will definitely take your efforts into account in deciding whether you must pay damages to a complainant. In fact, the courts and regulatory agencies encourage employers to take the initiative in correcting discriminatory hiring practices.

Here are some things you can do to show the courts and regulators that you're trying to make up for past discrimination in hiring:

1. Actively try to abolish discriminatory hiring practices as soon as the EEOC or another regulatory agency brings them to your attention.
2. Voluntarily adopt hiring standards that aim to correct past discriminatory policies.
3. Voluntarily eliminate tests and educational requirements that may have discriminated against some groups of applicants.
4. Start up your own affirmative-action program (see Chapter 9).

Notice to Applicants

One way to beat possible complainants to the punch is to show them that you know the law. And one way to do that is to let them know their rights under the law by posting highly visible notices in your personnel office and at other appropriate places throughout your organization.

Title VII. Along with posting EEOC-approved notices to advise job applicants of their rights under the antidiscrimination laws, you need to put up a notice that tells applicants how and where to file charges of discrimination in hiring.

Be sure to display Title VII notices in a prominent place—for example, a bulletin board where job postings usually appear. Intentional failure to put up notices where any and all can read them is punishable by fines of up to $100,000 per offense. Moreover, the courts and the EEOC may misconstrue such an act as evidence of a Title VII violation.

Executive Order 11246. Federal contractors and subcontractors must follow the same notice-posting dictates as private employers under Title VII. Posting EEOC-approved notices will satisfy the requirements of Executive Order 11246.

Age Discrimination in Employment Act. If this act applies to your business, you must post notices about the act that have been prepared and approved by the U.S. secretary of labor. You must place the notices in conspicuous spots throughout your workplace, and they must be easily accessible to applicants.

Equal Pay Act. You need to display posters that explain not only the equal-pay obligations for employers, but also requirements regarding overtime, minimum wages, and so on. Again, the notices must be conspicuously displayed.

Fair Credit Reporting Act. Even though you don't have to put up a public notice, this act requires you to inform a job applicant in writing if you run a credit check on him or her as a means of evaluating and verifying his or her qualifications.

Not discriminating in hiring is both the best defense *and* the best offense. If an applicant charges you with discriminatory hiring practices, you can prove to the courts and the regulators that you really didn't do anything wrong. If you do slip up, however, and the EEOC or a state regulatory agency comes sniffing around, the guidelines given in this chapter should help.

Of course, no defense is foolproof in a preemployment discrimination case. All the defenses described here are very subtle; it's easy to call the wrong play. But the right defense will probably deflect just about anything an applicant can dish out.

No matter which defense you use, keep this in mind:

**You can never use an exception to a rule
as an excuse for flagrantly breaking that rule.**

CHAPTER 9

AFFIRMATIVE-ACTION PROGRAMS

Employers can't discriminate against women and members of minority groups in hiring. But can they give preference to women and minorities in an attempt to turn the tables? Let's look at what the courts have to say:

• A white male applicant took a company to court because he claimed that its voluntary affirmative-action program, designed to benefit women and minorities, was an example of reverse discrimination.

The judge disagreed. The program was justified, he said, because the company had a demonstrable imbalance in its work force that reflected discrimination against minorities and women. He also noted that the existence of an affirmative-action program didn't mean that a company couldn't hire white men if it wanted to. After all, the program's objective was not to bar qualified candidates, but to rectify past abuses and achieve a more balanced work force in the short run.

• The EEOC ordered a midwestern city to implement an affirmative-action program to end long-standing discrimination in hiring against minorities and women. A group of white male applicants tried to challenge the program on the grounds of reverse discrimination, but the court firmly upheld the EEOC order.

The judge observed that Title VII of the Civil Rights Act of 1964 doesn't set any limits on what the EEOC can make employers do to curb racial discrimination in the workplace. So, if an employer establishes a reasonable affirmative-action program to correct discriminatory practices, that program is perfectly legal even though it may appear to step on the rights of white male applicants.

• A federal court ordered a local government agency to start hiring a disproportionate number of women and minority-group members to make up for discriminatory hiring practices in the past.

It's true that employment law gives employers the right to hire only the best-qualified candidate for the job, said the judge. But, he reasoned, employers also have a legal duty to correct discriminatory employment practices. It doesn't matter whether they simply inherited these practices from previous managers or whether they aggressively barred the door to women and members of minority groups. In the eyes of the courts and the regulators, discrimination is discrimination.

The message seems to be that you have a better chance of coming out ahead if a prospective employee sues you for reverse discrimination than if the EEOC sues you for discriminating against groups protected under Title VII. It's always smarter to follow the law even if you sympathize or identify with those hapless white male applicants who get left out in the cold. And sometimes the laws and regulations leave you no choice about giving female and minority applicants priority in hiring.

Obviously, paying lip service to the need for equal employment opportunity isn't enough to keep the EEOC and the courts off your back. If your company has a history of not exactly going out of its way to hire female and minority applicants, you might want to think about an affirmative-action program to give these groups more of a chance to participate in your work force. Of course, it's far better to initiate an affirmative-action program yourself than to have the EEOC or the courts order you to establish one.

TYPES OF PROGRAMS

All affirmative-action programs have the same goals:

1. To ensure that members of groups protected by Title VII are adequately represented at all levels of the work force.

2. To ensure that hiring practices are objective and administered fairly.

Affirmative-action programs do differ widely in scope and implementation, however.

Government-Ordered Programs

The federal government has actively intervened in its contractors' hiring practices since the 1960s. During that decade, various presidents issued executive orders that required federal contractors and their subcontractors to take a positive, continuing interest in eliminating discriminatory hiring practices.

Executive Order 11246 (as amended by Executive Order 11375) requires federal contractors and subcontractors to carry out in-house reviews to determine if their hiring practices are discriminatory. If they are, the contractor or subcontractor must take remedial action. For employers with 50 or more employees and federal contracts over $50,000, this means drawing up and implementing an affirmative-action program.

Court-Ordered Programs

Judges have imposed some extremely stringent affirmative-action programs in response to private discrimination suits, as well as to actions by the EEOC and other government agencies. The courts themselves administer these programs but may call on the EEOC to monitor them.

Voluntary Programs

Over the years, a growing number of progressive companies have acknowledged their social responsibilities to all sectors of society and have instituted affirmative-action programs on their own. In many instances, these programs are as effective as those the government mandates.

There are two real pluses to voluntary affirmative-action programs. First, the program offers irrefutable proof to the courts and regulators that the employer has complied with the equal-employment-opportunity laws in both letter *and* spirit. And if anyone challenges the program, the employer can certainly show that he or she has made a good-faith attempt to follow the law.

ANALYZING YOUR WORK FORCE

Before embarking on an affirmative-action program of your own (or preparing for a government-ordered one), you need to think about whether minority and female employees are underrepresented in your company's work force. Stay calm, keep a clear head, and take a logical, systematic approach to the problem.

Look at Your Workers

You should start your analysis by taking stock of who works for your company and what they do. You'll need to consider the following:

1. The minority groups represented in your company's work force (blacks, Hispanics, Asians, etc.).
2. The actual number of minority-group members and women holding jobs in your organization.
3. The classifications of the jobs these workers hold, and the concentration of female or minority workers in any position or at a certain level.
4. The number of positions held by minority-group members and women as a percentage of the entire work force.
5. The extent to which minority-group members and women are underrepresented in your company's work force.
6. Whether there is a sizable population of workers protected under Title VII in your area's labor pool.
7. The availability of minority and female applicants in the local work force who have the job skills your company needs.
8. The kinds of training resources that are available for newly hired employees and how your company might use them to upgrade the skills of female and minority employees.
9. How starting pay rates for women and minority-group members compare with pay scales for white male applicants.

Look at Your Hiring Practices

If an applicant sues you for discrimination in hiring, I can guarantee that the EEOC and the courts will zero in on your hiring practices first. Keep in mind, however, that the *consequences* of these practices determine whether they're discriminatory, not their intent.

To be sure that your hiring practices don't have discriminatory consequences, you should:

1. Analyze your recruitment procedures for each job category in the company.
2. Consider objective measures to monitor your hiring practices.
3. Keep records that identify each job applicant by name, race, age, sex, and so forth, and indicate whether you offered him or her a job.
4. Determine whether your recruiters and personnel staff are trained to apply objective hiring standards to all the applicants they deal with.
5. Give support to your company's existing affirmative-action programs.
6. Institute affirmative-action strategies for all positions in which women and minority-group members are underrepresented at your company.
7. Keep a list of promising minority and female candidates to consider for future openings.
8. Take an affirmative-action approach to your job advertising—think carefully about the type of ads you run, the media in which they appear, and so forth.
9. Place job orders with employment agencies that primarily serve members of minority groups.
10. Contact referral sources with access to qualified minority and female applicants.
11. Establish contacts with schools that have large minority enrollments.
12. Work closely with minority organizations to help train and equip their candidates for employment with your organization.

Look at Your Selection Standards

As I said in Chapter 4, the way you recruit and screen job applicants can get you into real trouble with the EEOC unless you're
careful. If you're serious about affirmative action, you have to put
your applicant selection standards under the microscope to make
sure they aren't discriminatory in any way. In fact, the EEOC requires employers to identify, analyze, and monitor every step of
the selection and hiring process to stave off possible adverse effects on groups protected under Title VII.

The EEOC employee selection guidelines forbid job qualifications or standards that disproportionately weed out prospective
employees protected under Title VII unless you can show that
these standards have something to do with job performance or
that no alternative selection standards are possible.

Not surprisingly, the EEOC and the courts tend to become
suspicious of tests, interview procedures, application forms, and
preemployment inquiries that lead to a high rate of rejection for
female and minority applicants. If you do use a test that might affect the employment status of a group protected under Title VII,
make sure you obtain proof from a qualified professional that the
test is an effective predictor of job performance.

Credit-check policies can also have a negative effect on minority hiring. If you turn down a minority applicant because of
his or her shaky credit record, you must be able to show that you
did it out of business necessity—that rejecting the prospective
employee was absolutely imperative to maintain the normal operation of your business. The same goes for arrest and conviction
records: You can't use them as a legal basis for rejecting an applicant unless you can prove that hiring a convicted felon would
endanger customers or otherwise disturb normal business operations in a big way.

Although I've talked mainly about female and minority-
group applicants so far, there's one other group you should be particularly sensitive to when you're evaluating your recruitment
and screening procedures for affirmative action: veterans. They're
protected by a couple of powerful laws:

1. The Veterans Reemployment Act of 1974 applies to all public and private employers. Under this act, if an employee

takes time off from his or her job to serve in the military or the National Guard, you must reinstate him or her without loss of status or benefits. The act also gives veterans the right to sue employers for violations.

2. The Vietnam-Era Veterans Readjustment Assistance Act applies to all employers with federal government contracts over $10,000. Enforced by the Department of Labor, the act requires contractors to take affirmative action to hire disabled Vietnam veterans.

REMOVING BARRIERS

If you identify obstacles to your efforts to implement an equal-employment-opportunity program, you might want to consider taking the following steps:

1. Make sure you and your staff base hiring decisions on a fair assessment of each applicant's employment history and background.
2. Develop and implement a formal employment evaluation program rooted in objective, quantifiable factors.
3. Require personnel managers to hire a certain percentage of qualified applicants in groups protected under Title VII.
4. Make it clear that members of protected groups are eligible for hiring on the basis of individual qualifications even if some positions have been traditionally filled by employees of a particular race or sex, or in a certain age group.
5. Target qualified members of protected groups for priority in hiring.
6. Set up a "remedial action file" of female and minority-group applicants that you and your staff can turn to first if there are any appropriate openings.
7. Establish career counseling programs for applicants and workers in protected groups.
8. Develop special training programs for female and minority-group applicants.
9. Don't refuse to hire female applicants because of female-

protective state laws that forbid women from working in hazardous industries or during "unsafe" hours.

10. Make sure minimum wage pay requirements for women set by state laws are equally applicable to men.

11. Apply the same standards to all employees that you call back to work after a layoff. Don't treat members of protected groups differently.

12. Don't try to cast blame on a union contract for your company's failure to take affirmative action.

13. Immediately change seniority systems that perpetuate discriminatory practices.

YOUR AFFIRMATIVE–ACTION POLICY

A company's commitment to an equal-employment-opportunity policy should come from the top, but it should specifically outline the responsibilities of each member of the staff involved in the hiring process.

After you've evaluated the composition of your company's work force and what you need to do to rectify any discriminatory policies, you're ready to launch your program. In the following sections, I'm going to give you some tips for getting the program off the ground and making sure it stays in the air.

Program Management

When possible, put *all* your affirmative-action policies in writing. Here's what good, comprehensive equal-employment-opportunity documentation should include:

Declaration of Intent. State that it is fundamental company policy to promote equal employment opportunities for all, regardless of race, sex, age, and so forth.

Statement of Affirmative Action. Note that your company is establishing special procedures to overcome the effects of prior discrimination.

Administration Responsibility. State that someone in a top management position will be responsible for making sure your equal-employment-opportunity program is effective.

Program Scope. Note that your affirmative-action plan will affect every aspect of your company's hiring process.

Program Description. Provide a complete and detailed narrative outlining the program's goals and operation.

Monitoring. State that you will establish an internal audit system to monitor the plan's effectiveness.

Evaluation Procedures. Indicate that the measurement and assessment tools for affirmative-action procedures will be similar to those used for other programs at your company.

When you're setting up an affirmative-action program, the community can be your best ally, especially if your company is located in an area with a large number of minority-group residents. Try to establish ties with influential community leaders and groups, and ask for their input on your plan.

Also, don't forget to review the plan with the EEOC or officials at a comparable state agency before and during implementation!

Publicity

To be effective, an affirmative-action plan must be "broadcast" both in-house and outside the company so that everyone who might be affected by the program knows about it. Here are some techniques you can use to publicize your company's program:

1. Describe the affirmative-action program in your personnel handbooks and manuals.
2. Post notices on company bulletin boards, as long as the notice is easily visible and the bulletin board isn't in a dark, secluded corner.
3. Brief managers and staff on the details of the program and their roles in its implementation.

4. Bring in consultants to help sell the program to workers who aren't members of protected groups.
5. Prepare brochures describing the program for personnel staff to hand out to job applicants.
6. Use company newsletters and other in-house publications to publicize and promote the program.
7. If your company is a union shop, enlist the union's help in spreading the word about the program and helping it to attain its objectives.

Goals and Timetables

You need to set realistic goals and equally realistic timetables for achieving them if your affirmative-action program is going to work.

A logical starting point is to knock down the most serious barriers to equal employment opportunity. Failure to take immediate action once you've identified discriminatory hiring practices can expose your company to private lawsuits, in addition to making it a sitting duck for an EEOC investigation. After you've taken care of these pressing obstacles to equal employment opportunity, tackle the discriminatory practices for which there are no easy, overnight solutions.

Whatever goals you set, make sure that they're realistic and that your company can achieve them without having to spend a lot of money or strain existing resources. Don't draw up an overly idealistic, pie-in-the-sky program that's doomed to failure.

Flexibility should be another hallmark of your program's goals. Equal-employment-opportunity laws change all the time, and you need to anticipate these changes and the effect they may have on your program. Make sure your goals and timetables can bend enough to accommodate changes in the law, as well as in the composition of the work force. Also, because the American economy is so competitive, goals and timetables should be able to expand or contract with your company's changing fortunes.

Just as your program encompasses the company as a whole, your goals and timetables should target the entire organization, not just one division or department. What's more, *all* employees must see it as fair—applicants and employees who aren't members of protected groups shouldn't perceive affirmative action as reverse discrimination.

Progress

To gauge whether the program is doing a good job of providing equal employment opportunity to every applicant, you need to review its policies, procedures, and practices from time to time. You should keep changes in the law and new EEOC regulations in mind whenever you evaluate or report on the progress of a program.

Always document your reviews to show that you've made a good-faith attempt to rectify past discrimination. Written reviews will come in handy for other reasons, too:

Reporting Requirements.   You'll need to prepare periodic reports that include the following items:

1. Studies you may have done of the company's work force according to race, sex, national origin, salary, wage level, and other variables.
2. A breakdown of the available labor pool by race, sex, and national origin.
3. Records that document each step of your hiring process.
4. Areas in which members of minority groups or women are underrepresented or concentrated.
5. A listing of referral sources.
6. Miscellaneous details and documents that support the progress your company has made.

Regulatory Audits.   Accountability is also critical when the EEOC comes around to check out your program and evaluate how it's doing. Here's what the EEOC will want to look at when it audits your affirmative-action program:

1. Your written description of the program and its implementation.
2. Your statement of policy and commitment to equal employment opportunity.
3. Your company's job application forms.

4. Your recruitment materials.
5. Your company handbooks, manuals, brochures, and bulletins.
6. Your testing and training materials.
7. The personnel department's track record and level of commitment to the program.
8. The composition of your work force by categories of groups protected under Title VII, and how these figures compare with work force statistics in general.
9. Your new hires for the last year, categorized by groups protected under Title VII.
10. Your view of the plan's progress.
11. Your involvement in discrimination-related litigation or an EEOC investigation.
12. Your analysis of the procedures and resources in place, to ensure success of the plan.

Community Involvement

As I mentioned earlier, without the support of the local community, you might find it tough to get your affirmative-action program going, much less ensure its success. Here are some hints for effective community relations:

1. When possible, involve the local community in the program to avoid potential hostility, misunderstandings, and resentment.
2. Consider supplying local applicants and workers with transportation to your worksite.
3. Think about setting up child care facilities.
4. Work hand-in-hand with local groups and institutions to provide education for potential applicants.
5. Provide training for workers in the community to upgrade their skills and qualifications.
6. Coordinate your efforts with local minority organizations.

FAIRNESS FOR ALL

Affirmative-action programs are *not* a means to create a self-perpetuating system of superiority for workers protected under Title VII. Employers and applicants alike should look on them simply as an attempt to replace discriminatory employment practices with nondiscriminatory ones.

Of course, if an affirmative-action program is improperly implemented or poorly run, a disgruntled applicant is likely to sue the company for reverse discrimination. If this happens, the courts and the EEOC will:

1. Check to see if the program actually evaluates the whole person for employment instead of just offering jobs automatically to applicants who belong to groups protected under Title VII.
2. Weigh the applicant's ability to relate to and communicate with a particular racial or ethnic group as a factor in the hiring decision, providing, of course, that such an ability is essential for the job in question.
3. Review the program to ensure that it complies with the nondiscriminatory tenets of Title VII.

A well-designed and well-administered affirmative-action program can keep the discrimination gremlins from your company's door, as well as help you to steer clear of problems with the EEOC. Instead of waiting passively for the courts or the government to impose such a program on you, it's far better to take the intiative to set up one of your own.

Keep these things in mind about affirmative action, and you'll be well on the way to doing it right:

The courts tend to look favorably on voluntary affirmative-action programs.

Title VII doesn't put any restraints on what an employer can do to correct racial discrimination in the workplace.

Plans aimed at eliminating racial imbalances in traditionally segregated jobs are still legal, despite the recent Supreme Court decision on reverse discrimination.

CHAPTER 10

TYING THE KNOT

You're almost at the end of the hiring trail. Your careful recruiting, screening, interviewing, and testing procedures have paid off. A winner has emerged from the pack, and you're all set to offer him or her a job with your company. The music swells, the credits roll. But are you and your prospective employee truly ready to ride off into the sunset together?

Sometimes employers forget that they have a contractual relationship with their applicants and employees. Whether or not it's on paper, the contract between an applicant and an employer begins as soon as the applicant accepts a job—and it's binding. The consequences of ignoring the employment contract can be disastrous for employers, as these examples demonstrate:

- When Thomas M. received a letter from Foobaron International to confirm that he'd been hired for an engineering position, he resigned from his old job and made plans to start at Foobaron in a week. For reasons unknown to Tom, however, Foobaron decided to transfer the entire engineering department to another state.

  During Tom's interview, the engineering manager had said that the company wasn't planning to relocate any of its departments. Because Tom couldn't just pick up and follow the department, he was out of a job. Needless to say, he was also furious, so he sued Foobaron for fraud and deceit . . . and won.

- Harriet J. left a sales job with a telephone company because it monitored employee calls, a practice she found offensive. When she applied for a similar position with another phone company, the department manager assured her that the company detested monitoring as much as she did.

Within a few weeks of starting her new job, however, Harriet learned that the company had decided to monitor the phones in her department. She asked for a transfer to another department, but the personnel office told her that no other jobs were available; she could keep working in the same department, or she could walk. She walked to the nearest court and filed a breach-of-contract action against the company.

• A Philadelphia bank offered Allen C. a job. He accepted on the condition that he not be required to work on Saturdays; as he told the interviewer, he celebrated the Sabbath on Saturday. But after Allen had been on the job two months, his supervisor said he'd have to work Saturdays, or else. When Allen refused, he was fired. He wasted no time in filing a wrongful-discharge suit.

Obviously, hiring right doesn't end with an offer of employment. In this chapter, I'll cover what to include in your written or verbal employment contracts so that you don't get more than you bargain for when you make a job offer.

HOW EMPLOYMENT CONTRACTS WORK

Inherent in all employment relationships, the employment contract comes into being when you make a verbal or written job offer to an applicant. Believe me, the courts *will* enforce this contract; it doesn't matter whether the agreement is expressed or implied.

The employment contract sets the terms of the relationship between employer and employee. When you're ready to offer a job to a promising applicant, you need to couch that offer in exactly the right terms: Your goal is to ensure that there are absolutely no questions about what you expect from prospective employees. Therefore, you must detail your terms and conditions as soon as you know you've got a live one on the line.

If the prospective employee signs an actual employment contract, everything's easy as long as the agreement lays out your terms. If you forget something, just make sure the contract refers to personnel handbooks and other materials that govern conditions of employment when the applicant becomes an employee of your company.

When there is no written agreement to summarize the employment relationship, you should make it clear during interviews and in any correspondence with applicants that they must abide by your terms of employment on accepting a job with your company.

Here are some other crucial elements to watch out for when you make a job offer:

Proxies

In some cases, the person you offer a job to may not be the person who actually reports to work! To prevent applicants from bringing in proxies to work for them once they've been hired, point out that you're offering the job only to the applicant, not to his or her friends and relatives. Job offers aren't transferable.

Expected Duties

Give the prospective emplyee a complete job description—in writing, if possible. As far as duties are concerned, it doesn't really matter whether you have a written or verbal agreement to cement the employment relationship.

Minority and female employees often complain that white male workers with the same job description do less demanding tasks. Outlining the duties of the job in question gives everyone a clear reference point and defuses charges of discrimination.

Location

Many an applicant has accepted an offer to work in the Sun Belt only to learn after coming on board that he or she will actually be working in a different and far less attractive part of the country. In fact, women and members of minority groups have charged employers with using assignments to remote, undesirable job locations as a subtle way of driving them out of the work force.

Geography doesn't have to lead to hiring problems if you use common sense and tell your new employees exactly where they'll be working. Let applicants know in advance where the plant is located, which regions their territory will cover, or where they're likely to be traveling on business, and they'll have no reason to whine about having to spend half the year in East Podunk.

Compensation

The antidiscrimination laws make no bones about it: Employees who do the same job must receive the same salary and other compensation. Religion, sex, and race can't influence pay scales.

Charges of discrimination often center on inequities in pay, benefits, vacation time, and other forms of compensation. To deflect possible discrimination charges, be up-front with prospective employees about their salary and benefits. Also, be sure to stress that experience and qualifications determine whether workers get paid higher starting salaries, not race, sex, or religion.

Religious Observances

Christianity may be the dominant religion in the United States, but it's certainly not the only one. We live in a pluralistic society with freedom of religion guaranteed in our laws from the Constitution on down. Unfortunately, an employer's ideas of when an employee should work may clash with an employee's ideas of when he or she should worship or celebrate a religious holiday.

If your company's operations require employees to work on weekends or holidays, let job applicants know from the start. "Forgetting" to tell a Seventh-Day Adventist that he or she must work on Saturdays could result in charges of religious discrimination. On the other hand, you're not under any obligation ot hire someone who refuses or is unable to do the job as described during the preemployment stage.

When you offer a job to an applicant, give him or her a list of your company's paid holidays. If the applicant requests time off with pay to observe a religious holiday that's not on the list, you should grant the request if other employees have the same privilege.

As pointed out previously, a reasonable attempt to accommodate your employees' religious observances is all the law demands. But if you let your Jewish employees take Rosh Hashanah and Yom Kippur off with pay, you must give members of other religious groups in your work force time off with pay for *their* holidays.

A good rule of thumb is that an employee should receive paid time off only for holidays specified during the interview period. If the employee wants to take time off for other, nonspecified holidays, he or she will probably have to dip into personal or vacation time.

Sick Leave

Let job applicants know your sick-leave policy to give them an idea of how your company might deal with catastrophic illnesses such as cancer or AIDS. If you put your sick-leave policy in writing and apply it to all employees across the board, you should be able to stave off charges of discrimination under the Federal Rehabilitation Act and similar state laws.

Maternity Leave

Pregnancy is a medical condition under federal and state laws, which forbid you from firing a pregnant employee or refusing to hire a pregnant applicant. When it comes to maternity leave policy, however, the law isn't quite as clear-cut. You aren't obligated to hold a pregnant employee's job for her until she returns from maternity leave (although some companies do). But you are obligated to find her an equally suitable job at the same rate of pay.

Whatever maternity leave policy you decide on, make sure you describe every facet of it in your written or verbal employment contract. An ambiguous maternity policy is a front-row ticket to a sex-discrimination suit.

Insurance Coverage

Federal and state laws make it illegal to deny medical disability or life insurance coverage to older employees. You can't discriminate against them by offering lower premiums and better coverage to younger employees.

Your company's insurance program cannot discriminate on the basis of race or sex either. Don't let minority workers accuse you of giving white employees an insurance break because mortality figures for members of minority groups are reportedly higher than those for whites.

Ownership of Work Product

You have the right to ask prospective employees to turn over any inventions (or their patents) that they develop while working for your company. You can bundle this request into your written or verbal employment contract or put it in a separate agreement. But you can't demand that only prospective employees of one religion, sex, or ethnic group sign such agreements.

Illegal Activity

When you make an offer, you have the authority to ask prospective employees not to steal or commit other illegal acts at the workplace, and to require them to notify the appropriate department if they witness anything illegal on the job. These are perfectly legitimate and justifiable conditions of employment.

Some people have honor codes that consider loyalty to friends the paramount virtue: To "rat" on a colleague is the worst crime one can commit. If you run across an applicant who refuses to let company officials know if a fellow employee does something illegal, you can retract the job offer.

Employee Searches

The law wants you to protect your company against illegal activities such as workplace drug use and employee thievery. One step you can take to curb these problems is to encourage employees to allow searches of their desks, lockers, and other company property *for good cause*. As a condition of employment, you can ask prospective employees to agree to such searches, providing they aren't discriminatory or abusive. Make sure applicants understand why you might need to search and why they should agree to employee searches. And get their permission in writing!

Noncompete Agreements

The courts have upheld the right to ask a prospective employee to sign a noncompete agreement, which prevents him or her from working for a competitor or setting up a directly competitive business for a certain period after resigning from your company.

You won't get into trouble if you have applicants sign a noncompete agreement as a condition of employment, as long as you limit the geographic area the agreement covers and keep its duration reasonable. For instance, if your noncompete agreement prevents employees from working for direct competitors within a radius of 100 miles for up to three years after leaving the company, it will probably stand up in court.

As you might expect, you can't use a noncompete agreement to bar an employee from working for an unrelated industry or a company that isn't a direct competitor of your firm.

Basis for Termination

Even though you're about to embark on what you hope will be a mutually rewarding partnership between your company and the prospective employee, you can't forget about the dark side of employment. Hiring, as you know, may eventually lead to firing, no matter how promising the candidate.

What you want to avoid at all costs is wrongful discharge litigation. Therefore, it's a good idea to tell prospective employees about the kinds of behavior and activities that your company considers grounds for termination. Actually, you *must* identify these grounds at the preemployment stage; the courts could well view your firing criteria as arbitrary and biased if you don't explain them to an employee until you're ready to give him or her the ax.

Severance

The U.S. economy isn't exactly the Rock of Gibraltar, especially in the high-tech and manufacturing sectors. Now that layoffs have become a sad but inevitable part of the American work scene, you should be careful to tell applicants about your company's severance policies. If your company must lay off part of its work force, alerting prospective employees about your severance policies in advance will deflate charges that the company laid off women and members of minority groups before other workers.

Dispute Resolution

If your company has in-house vehicles for resolving or arbitrating disputes between management and workers, explain the process to prospective employees. This is especially important if the workplace is unionized.

Also, if you use a written employment contract, make sure it specifies which state laws will apply to disputes between your company and the employee, as well as the methods to be used in resolving problems. For example, your contract might state that all disputes will be resolved by arbitration under the laws of New Jersey.

UNENFORCEABLE EMPLOYMENT AGREEMENTS

Written employment agreements have obvious merits, but the courts won't uphold them automatically just because they're on paper. As I said earlier, an employment contract can be verbal, too; if there isn't a written agreement, the courts can construe an employment contract from statements and other relevant materials. And a verbal contract can be just as valid as a written one.

Whether it's written or verbal, however, an employment agreement must meet certain criteria to be enforced by the courts.

For instance, the courts are aware that employers have more bargaining power than job applicants; they know that employment is a seller's market. Therefore, they won't uphold an agreement that an employer has forced down a prospective employee's throat, such as a "take it or leave it" job offer or one of those offers a prospective employee "just can't refuse."

When bargaining with a prospective employee, employers are expected to be candid and forthright. If the employer uses fraud or trickery to induce the applicant to come on board or if the offer was precipitated by economic pressure or duress, the employment contract won't stand up in court.

Obviously, an employment contract cannot require an employee to do anything that's illegal or unethical. For example, a firm can't demand that a female executive "specialize" in male clients because such a request would run afoul of the sex-discrimination laws and the courts would undoubtedly strike it down.

Likewise, an employment contract cannot ask a prospective employee to go along with discrimination in the workplace. A company that refuses to hire Chicanos cannot fire a manager who won't follow this blatantly discriminatory policy, which violates Title VII and just about every other employment law described in this book.

In general, an enforceable employment agreement must have reasonable objectives. You can't expect your prospective employees to hop every time your company says frog, and you can't use the employment contract to punish them for joining a union or not seeing things your way. But employment is a two-way street: The well-tuned contract works to your advantage, too, because it lets the employee know exactly where you stand and minimizes threats of litigation.

THE HIRING LETTER

In many cases, companies don't have prospective employees sign contracts, but they do send out hiring letters to confirm a previous offer of employment or an applicant's acceptance of an employment offer. More and more courts are giving hiring letters the same weight as actual employment contracts.

A poorly drafted hiring letter could come back to haunt you in the form of a wrongful discharge suit or breach-of-contract action. To protect yourself, follow these guidelines in composing your letter:

1. Ensure that everything you say is accurate, and don't make any overt or implied promises that you're unwilling or unable to keep.
2. Precisely define the parameters of the job in question—the terms of employment, pay rate, start date, and so forth.
3. Refer to your company's internal personnel policies, and describe how they govern the employer-employee relationship. If the personnel handbook isn't too voluminous, enclose a copy with the hiring letter, and state in the letter that its policies are binding on acceptance of the job offer.
4. Remember that such expressions as "delighted by your acceptance" can seem like more than politeness in court. For example, if your letter states, "We look forward to a long and happy relationship with you, " the court might interpret the sentence to mean that you've promised the applicant long-term employment.
5. Likewise, don't guarantee job satisfaction ("We know you'll be happy working for XYZ International") because it can be turned against you in a breach-of-contract lawsuit. A disgruntled employee can argue that you failed to live up to your guarantees.
6. When possible, don't promise the prospective employee chances for advancement, more money, or better benefits in

your letter. A court could force you to honor these promises if the employee sues you down the line. Remember: In deciding whether to enforce a hiring letter, an arbitrator or judge will look at discrepancies between the contents of the letter and the employee's actual day-to-day work conditions.

7. If the letter is an alternative to a full-blown employment contract, be sure to include all the specifics of the employment relationship. Treat the hiring letter as if it *were* an employment contract.

8. Always request the prospective employee to sign (execute) and return the hiring letter to you before reporting for work. If the employee signs it after starting work, at least some of the conditions set out in the letter may be waived.

CONFIDENTIALITY AGREEMENTS

If a prospective employee will have access to confidential business secrets and other valuable proprietary information, it's a good idea to have him or her sign a confidentiality or nondisclosure agreement before he or she comes on board.

Confidentiality agreements are an effective and inexpensive way to guard your company's priceless trade secrets against dishonest employees and corporate spies. They're perfectly legal, and the courts usually won't perceive them as discriminatory unless the employer asks only members of specific groups to sign them.

Confidentiality agreements have two key functions. They let prospective employees know that if they accept employment with your company they must not disclose any of its trade secrets or other confidential information. They also transfer liability for misuse of business secrets from the company to its employees: An employee who spills a trade secret must assume legal responsibility for any loss that he or she causes the company.

To be truly airtight, however, a confidentiality agreement must:

1. Specifically outline what's expected of employees who deal with confidential information.

2. Spell out exactly what constitutes misuse of business secrets by employees.
3. Note that the employee executed the agreement knowingly and willingly.

Although their content will vary from employer to employer, all confidentiality agreements should:

1. Define "proprietary information" as specifically as possible, and make sure the definition covers any modifications or changes to the information.
2. Define "authorized and proper use" of proprietary information.
3. Describe all legal uses of the information.
4. Require the employee to return all proprietary information to the company on leaving his or her job.
5. Describe the employee's duties and obligations concerning the handling of the information.
6. Require the employee to assume a legal obligation for any losses resulting from his or her breach of the agreement.

Of course, you don't want your confidentiality agreement to seem discriminatory or to go against public policy, so make sure that the agreement complies with both federal and state employment laws, doesn't appear to single out any group or individual, and is in line with in-house personnel policies and, if applicable, collective bargaining pacts. Also, each prospective employee should get a copy of it in advance, so he or she can review it with a lawyer.

HIRING INDEPENDENT CONTRACTORS

Most employees work for wages under an employer's direct or indirect supervision. An independent contractor, however, takes on a job for a set fee, often payable in installments, and maintains the right to decide how the job will be performed—for instance, whether he or she will do the work or subcontract it to someone else. Also, an independent contractor usually (but not always) has a written contract with the person or company who hires him or her.

Drafting an agreement for the services of an independent contractor can be tricky. To limit your legal exposure when working with independent contractors, define your needs and the services you want the contractor to perform *before* hiring him or her. Also, because many hassles with independent contractors involve missed deadlines, make sure the contract contains a schedule that specifies the work to be done and the time frame for doing it. Stipulate that you must approve all changes to this schedule in writing.

Although the law places strict boundaries on what employers can do to screen prospective employees, it doesn't have nearly as much to say about screening to hire independent contractors. You still want to hire right, however, so here are some tips:

1. Check out the qualifications of the contractor and the members of his or her staff who will be working on the project. Don't forget about subcontractors, either!
2. Confirm the contractor's level of expertise and past job performance.
3. Get in touch with the contractor's references, and also check with his or her previous clients.
4. Interview the key members of the contractor's staff who will be working on the project.
5. Check out the contractor's liability coverage.
6. Do a credit check to determine if the contractor has been sued by creditors, customers, or others.

You're within your rights if you want to screen your independent contractors. In fact, you *should* screen a contractor as carefully and thoroughly as you screen your full-time employees.

Money is the root of much litigation between independent contractors and those who hire them. To forestall fee-related problems, make sure the contract:

1. Gives the hourly or daily fee that you will pay to the contractor.
2. Lists any hidden charges the contractor may pass on to you.
3. Specifies financial penalties you will assess if the contractor fails to provide services on schedule.

4. States who is responsible for taxes and other costs connected with the project.

Independent contractors often go to court to prove that they actually own what they produced even though it was "work for hire" performed for someone else. Usually, an ambiguous contract is the source of such confusion, so your agreement should specify that you own an inventions, programs, books, or other products resulting from the contractor's work for you.

Never believe for one minute that contractors will keep a secret, no matter what kind of sterling reputations they may have. In fact, contractors have even less of a vested interest in maintaining the confidentiality of trade secrets than "regular" employees. That's why you should ask all your independent contractors to sign confidentiality agreements if they're going to be seeing or working with sensitive proprietary information.

Because you can be held liable for the acts of your contractor just as if he or she were a full-time employee, make sure your contract holds the contractor legally responsible for problems, defects, and losses caused by his or her errors. You might also think about asking the contractor to post a bond.

The contractor is working for you, so you should have ultimate authority over all changes to the work contract; before the contractor makes a change, require your approval in writing. Also, any agreement with an independent contractor should specify the process and applicable state laws for resolving disputes.

Independent contractor is a fuzzy term under the law; the label itself isn't enough to determine whether an individual is actually an independent contractor or is working on a fee-for-service basis. The litmus test the courts use is whether an employer intrudes on the worker's right to carry out the job any way he or she wants to. The more an employer has to say about how the job is done, the more likely the courts will consider the worker an employee rather than an independent contractor. Thus, your actions, as well as the contract, influence how the courts view the arrangement.

HIRING FOR THE WRONG REASONS

Even the most carefully wrought employment contract won't keep you out of court if you don't hire right in the first place.

All too often, a company will offer a job to an applicant because it fears that a competitor will hire him or her first, not because the company has any real need for the applicant's talents. When officials leave government posts, for instance, companies usually scramble to hire them, and it's not that federal employees make such dedicated and wonderful workers in the private sector. Rather, companies feel that they have to snap these employees up before the competition so that they can gain an edge in dealing with the government agencies these employees used to work for.

Actually, hiring someone because he or she has connections to a government agency your company does business with can be hazardous to your legal health. If you ever have to let the employee go, you could be up for a wrongful discharge suit, especially if you promised employment security to induce the applicant to accept the job.

Even though company growth and industry trends are hard to predict, companies prefer to err on the side of optimism. As a result, they may take on more workers than they actually need to meet the demands of expected growth. But optimistic overhiring can be dangerous if the growth curve flattens out and the company has to lay off all those workers.

Putting on rose-colored glasses to examine hiring needs is bad enough. What's worse is when companies hire because of *perceived* rather than real needs. For example, a manager may think an applicant knows something the company can't live without, so the manager rushes to hire the applicant before someone else grabs him or her.

Because such hiring decisions are rooted in unreality, they're generally doomed to failure. Worse, if you try to correct this kind of hiring mistake by letting the employee go, the courts are likely to be on the employee's side. You could find yourself staring down the barrel of an emotional-distress suit.

Employers who hire applicants simply because they possess highly specialized skills that the employer needs for a short time can also wind up in court. Typically, the employee tells the company about the specialized skill, and the company essentially throws him or her away after taking advantage of it. Of course, you can light the powder keg yourself if you promise long-term employment to such workers.

Then there are employers who fall in love with big names.

They think that by hiring an industry honcho they'll automatically run the rest of the industry into the ground. Unfortunately, when you hire a star, you hire his or her overblown ego, too—and it's very easy to trample on an ego and end up in court. Also, you'll find that stars are hard to control or manage.

No matter whom you hire, don't forget the cardinal rule of employment law:

> **The employment contract is binding, and it begins when you offer an applicant a job.**

An employment agreement can be a written contract, a hiring letter, or even a handshake after an interview—as long as it documents the conditions of employment and finalizes the employer-employee relationship. You shouldn't have any trouble with breach-of-contract or discrimination suits involving your employment agreements if you follow this suggestion:

> **Tell prospective employees, preferably in writing, what you expect of them before they come on board.**

CHAPTER 11

FOR THE RECORD

Did you know that there are laws requiring you to hang on to a job applicant's records for a fixed period of time even if you don't hire that person? "Oh, come on, " you might scoff. "I can see the point of maintaining records for the people I hire . . . but why should I care about the paperwork for the ones who don't make it?"

If you've learned just one thing from this book, it's that the ones who don't make it are the ones who are most likely to give you legal headaches. And if a disgruntled job applicant does sue you, failure to produce hiring-related records when the courts or regulators ask for them can get you into a real jam:

• Fifty-eight-year-old Bob K. applied for a job with an Oregon electronics firm. He suffered through several grueling tests and an equally excruciating interview only to learn that a younger applicant had been picked for the job. A few weeks after receiving the bad news, Bob filed an age-discrimination complaint with the EEOC, which asked the electronics company to turn over his application records.

The company told the EEOC that it had destroyed Bob's file because he was no longer under active consideration for employment. The EEOC official in charge of the suit merely replied that under the Age Discrimination in Employment Act employers must keep such records for at least one year. He added that the company's failure to hold on to the records for the minimum period would most certainly enter into the agency's decision on the case.

• Nancy F. applied for a management position with a national hotel franchise, but the job went to a less qualified male applicant. Nancy sued the hotel chain for sexual discrimination. The company told the judge that it had destroyed Nancy's application form and other relevant records. The judge's response was swift and simple: He ruled in Nancy's favor.

• When agents of the U.S. Immigration and Naturalization Service paid a visit to the offices of a Virginia construction firm, the manager couldn't produce Employment Eligibility and Verification (I-9) forms for several employees, nor could he provide any documents to establish their identity. Before they left, the agents told the manager that he had three days to locate the required records. If he didn't come up with what the agents wanted, his company would face some heavy penalties.

Applicant recordkeeping, like all recordkeeping, is a hassle. But you'll have to agree that maintaining applicant records is infinitely less of a hassle than losing a lawsuit because you can't produce the right piece of paper, or having the EEOC slap nasty sanctions on your company because you didn't think you had to hold on to a particular file. This chapter, which summarizes recordkeeping requirements for job applicants and employees under the major employment laws, should help you get your filing cabinets in good order.

FAIR LABOR STANDARDS ACT

The Fair Labor Standards Act (FLSA) imposes a sometimes confusing array of recordkeeping demands on employers. Many FLSA requirements concern various aspects of the hiring process, so you need to pay close attention to them.

New Employees

Employers subject to the FLSA's minimum wage and/or overtime provisions (and that's just about all employers) must maintain the following information for every new employee:

1. Full name (for social security purposes).
2. Home address.
3. Date of birth (if the employee is younger than 19).
4. Workweek schedule and hourly wage to be paid.

5. Number of work hours per week.
6. Total overtime compensation due for the workweek.
7. Total wages paid in any pay period.

It's pretty likely that you'll have to maintain at least these records for every person you hire. If your new employees are subject to the FLSA's equal-pay provisions, you'll also have to preserve any and all business records that might explain a wage differential for members of one sex or the other—pay figures, job evaluations, and the like.

Minors

Under the FLSA's child labor provisions, employers who hire minors must ask them to produce an *unexpired* certificate of age. This is particularly important if the minor maintains that he or she is a year older than the minimum age for the job in question or if physical appearance indicates that a minor is younger than the applicable minimum age.

The certificate of age should contain the following information:

1. The minor's name and address.
2. His or her place and date of birth, sex, and signature.
3. The name(s) and address(es) of the minor's parents or guardians.
4. The employer's name and address (if the minor is under 18).
5. The minor's occupation (if he or she is under 18).
6. The signature of the officer that issued the certificate, and the date and place of issuance.

The employer must also retain a record of the minor's birth date for at least three years.

Executives and Professionals

Under the FLSA, your records on workers hired for bona fide executive or professional positions should include at least this information:

1. The employee's name and address.
2. His or her place and date of birth, sex, and signature.
3. The name and address of his or her parents.

In addition, you must also keep a record of the system or basis you use for paying executives and professional workers, and of the total remuneration they receive for each pay period, including fringe benefits.

Maintaining FLSA Records

The FLSA requires you to retain some records for at least three years, including:

1. All payroll records.
2. Employment contracts.
3. Collective bargaining agreements.
4. Written agreements summarizing the terms of verbal agreements or understandings.

In addition, the FLSA requires you to hang on to these records for at least two years:

1. All time cards.
2. Earning records.
3. Records used to compute wages or salaries.
4. Overtime records.
5. Records establishing hours and days of employment.
6. Records that explain the basis for any pay differentials.

AGE DISCRIMINATION IN EMPLOYMENT ACT

If you're not sitting on payroll records for at least three years to fulfill FLSA requirements, you'll probably have to maintain them anyway to satisfy the Age Discrimination in Employment Act. Your records must contain each employee's name, address, date of birth, pay scale, weekly compensation, and occupation.

The Age Discrimination in Employment Act also requires you to retain these applicant and employee records for at least one year:

1. Job application forms.
2. Résumés.
3. Communications with employment agencies.
4. Recruitment information.
5. Job advertisements and notices of employment.
6. Applicants' test records.
7. Records of physical and psychological exams connected to hiring decisions.
8. Records dealing with seniority systems.
9. Promotion records.
10. Records of selection criteria for training.

The one-year retention period doesn't apply to application forms and other preemployment records for temporary positions, as long as applicants are aware that such jobs are temporary before they're hired.

TITLE VII

Although the EEOC doesn't have any specific rules concerning retention of hiring records, it does have the authority to make employers hold on to such records, especially if it suspects an employer of discriminatory hiring practices.

If your company has 100 or more employees, you must file copies of Employer Information Report EEO-1 with the EEOC or a delegated agency. Report EEO-1 requires a company to record the racial and ethnic composition of its work force. But if a company does gather statistics on its workers' racial or ethnic identity for the purpose of completing Report EEO-1, it must maintain this information separately from its employees' basic personnel files or other personnel records. The EEOC might perceive failure to keep racial information out of personnel records as evidence of discrimination.

The EEOC requires you to retain the following records for at least six months from the time they were prepared:

1. All records related to hiring.
2. Application forms.
3. Termination records.

4. Records dealing with pay scales or terms of compensation.
5. Records of selection criteria for training.

Title VII also indirectly authorizes the EEOC to require employers to maintain records of involuntary termination for at least six months after the employee is fired.

Discrimination Charges

If the EEOC or your local human rights commission investigates a job applicant's charges of discrimination, you must hold on to every conceivable scrap of paper related to the charges until the case is resolved. That means *all* records, including:

1. The complainant's personnel records.
2. Records for other employees holding positions similar to the one the complainant applied for.
3. Application forms or test results for others who went after the same job as the complainant.

Likewise, if an apprentice files a discrimination suit, you must retain his or her application forms, test results, and other pertinent records for at least three years.

GOVERNMENT CONTRACTORS

The U.S. government, as we all know, is very keen on records, so it should come as no surprise that employers who do business with the federal government have even more recordkeeping demands to deal with than private-sector employers. But it's for a good cause: The government uses these records to evaluate its contractors' compliance with the equal-employment-opportunity laws.

Public Contracts Act

Under this act, any employer who contracts with the federal government to manufacture or furnish materials, supplies, articles, or equipment must maintain the following records for at least three years from the last date of entry for every employee:

1. The employee's name, address, sex, and occupation.
2. Date of birth (if the employee is younger than 19).
3. Payroll records, including wage rates and amount paid during each pay period.

The Public Contracts Act also stipulates that federal contractors maintain the following information for at least two years from the last date of entry or the last effective date of the records, whichever is later:

1. All time and earning cards.
2. Any tables or schedules used by the employer.
3. All schedules establishing hours and days of employment.

Service Contract Act

This act requires any employer who makes a contract with a federal agency for more than $2,500 to keep the following records for at least three years from the date the contract work is completed:

1. Each employee's name and address.
2. Work classifications and rates of pay for each employee.
3. Number of daily and weekly hours worked.
4. Refunds or deductions from the total compensation for each worker employed under the contract.
5. Monetary fringe benefits for employees not covered by the minimum-wage attachment to the contract.

Apprentices and Trainees

Federal contractors and subcontractors holding contracts of more than $2,500 must maintain records for all apprentices and trainees hired for federally assisted construction programs. The required information includes:

1. The number, by trade, of apprentices and trainees working under the contract.
2. Wages paid and hours worked by each apprentice or trainee.
3. Name, address, date of birth, fringe benefits, and so on for each apprentice or trainee.

DISCLOSING PERSONNEL RECORDS

Once you have all this information about job applicants and employees sitting around for several years, what do you do when someone other than a judge or an EEOC official asks to take a look at it?

You probably get umpteen requests a day for information about job applicants or former employees. By now, you're probably wondering when—if ever—you should give out such sensitive information to others.

Naturally, there are some legitimate circumstances for disclosing your personnel records. In general, you can make information about job applicants or former employees available to third parties if the information affects an important interest of your company and if its disclosure will help you protect that interest.

As the courts interpret it, an "important interest" can involve one or more of these things:

1. A legal duty to disclose the information.
2. Compliance with court orders or regulatory agency requests.
3. The need to defend your company's reputation.
4. The desire to expose or warn others about an employee's misconduct. (This is an acceptable interest as long as the warning is factual and not defamatory.)
5. The need to protect your business against unfair competition.
6. The need to protect the interests of third parties.
7. The need to further some public policy or interest.

How to Get into Trouble

As you might expect, you can't unconditionally broadcast information about a job applicant or former employee to the world. In fact, an employer's right to make personnel records available to others will go up in smoke if:

1. The employer doesn't believe that the information he or she is disclosing is true.

2. The employer doesn't have a reasonable basis for supporting the accuracy of the information.
3. The employer gives out the information for other than legitimate business reasons.
4. The information the employer provides isn't what the third party has asked for.
5. The employer uses the disclosure as a way of harming the applicant or former employee.
6. The employer discloses sensitive information out of malice, hatred, or vindictiveness.
7. The employer makes the disclosure through an improper channel.
8. The disclosure is an obvious show of bad faith on the part of the employer.

Protecting Yourself

It may seem as if you're automatically going to land in a legal snakepit if you give out information in your records on applicants and former employees. As is true of everything else in employment law, however, a little common sense and forethought go a long way.

Here are some suggestions for limiting your legal liability when you want to disclose personnel information:

1. Review the information you're disclosing to ensure that you're not sending out anything that could be grounds for a lawsuit.
2. Let the applicant or former employee know that you're planning to release information about him or her.
3. When possible, have the applicant or former employee sign a release consenting to the disclosure.
4. Tell employees who want to use you as a reference that the information you provide will be candid and factual.
5. Make sure the person who asks for sensitive personnel information is who he or she claims to be.
6. Ask the person requesting the information to provide a written authorization for his or her request.
7. Check to see if the applicant or employee has put any limitations on the information your company can give out about him or her.

8. Handle all disclosures in a businesslike manner.
9. Never supply information that the person making the request hasn't asked for.

When you are dealing with applicant and employee records, don't forget this all-important rule:

**The law requires you to hold on to many
personnel records for at least two or three years.**

When you've accumulated the records you need to keep the EEOC and the courts happy, keep this in mind when others ask you for them:

**Don't give anything away unless there's
a legitimate business reason for
the disclosure.**

CHAPTER 12

WHAT COMES NEXT?

One word sums up hiring in the 1980s: *regulation.*

I wrote this book to help you make sense of the laws, rules, and judicial decisions that govern the hiring process. If you know the law, you'll be less likely to flaunt it, and you'll be able to defend yourself if a disgruntled job applicant goes on the warpath and sues you for discriminatory hiring practices.

Probably the most useful insight I can give you, however, is an awareness of how regulated the American employment process is today. From the Department of Labor to your local human rights commission, regulators tell you how to recruit, screen, test, interview, and offer jobs to prospective employees. The fact is, you share all your hiring decisions with the government. You may not like it, but if you want to avoid problems, you live with it. Believe me, the hot water you get into when you violate government regulations is no Jacuzzi!

Don't expect the regulators to lighten up, either. If I read the legislative clues correctly, we're in for a lot more government intervention in employment during the 1990s.

Throughout this book, I've told you to keep up with antidiscrimination regulations and other laws that affect your company's hiring practices if you want to avoid legal problems. With the government opening up equal employment opportunity to more groups while simultaneously clamping down on employers' rights to test and screen applicants, that advice is going to become even more valid over the next decade.

EXPANDED PROTECTION

Under current antidiscrimination laws, employers must be blind to an applicant's color, race, sex, religion, ethnic group, and national origin when they hire. Some groups believe even this coverage doesn't go far enough, however, and are pushing for Congress and the state legislatures to broaden the antidiscrimination laws to include applicants and workers who've never enjoyed such protection before.

Catastrophic Illnesses

If the dire predictions about AIDS come true, this terrible disease will become the Black Death of the 1990s. Even if a cure is found tomorrow, the virus's period of latency is so long that AIDS will continue to have a profound impact on the American work force throughout that decade at least.

In some areas, it's illegal to discriminate against a job applicant with a catastrophic illness. Although most of these local ordinances were designed to protect people with AIDS and AIDS-related complex, Congress and the states are considering expanding the antidiscrimination laws to include individuals with cancer and other serious diseases.

New drugs and, in a few happy instances, cures are prolonging the lives of many people with catastrophic illnesses and allowing them to be productive members of the work force. If the present crop of bills relating to workers with serious diseases become state or federal laws, employers will find it tough to justify any opposition to them.

Alternative Lifestyles

AIDS has devastated the gay community. Not surprisingly, many gay activists have channeled their advocacy and lobbying efforts into increased legal protection for people with AIDS and ARC. But that doesn't mean gay and lesbian civil rights have fallen off the activist agenda.

As I've said before, Title VII of the Civil Rights Act of 1964 doesn't guarantee employment rights for homosexuals. Gay activists, however, are urging Congress to expand the law to include workers with "alternative lifestyles." If that happens, employers won't be able to use sexual orientation as a rationale for refusing employment to male homosexuals and lesbians. Sexual preference will join race, religion, and national origin as a variable that cannot influence hiring decisions in any way, and gays and lesbians will be able to sue employers for discriminatory hiring practices. Gay civil rights bills that would give homosexuals similar protection in hiring are also wending their way through several state legislatures.

Right now, AIDS remains a priority issue for legislators as well as gays. But Congress and the states may well turn their attention to protecting the employment rights of homosexuals if AIDS ceases to be a national emergency.

Developmental Disabilities

Few of us give the mentally retarded credit for being employable, but not every person with a developmental disability is so severely retarded that he or she cannot function independently. More and more companies are learning that developmentally disabled adults can become loyal, able workers under the right conditions.

Efforts are afoot at the federal and local levels to close existing legal loopholes that make it possible for employers to bar developmentally disabled applicants from the workplace. Such legislation has been percolating through Congress for awhile, and it looks as if something may actually happen over the next few years. It's a situation that certainly bears watching.

TESTING TRENDS

In April 1989, the Exxon supertanker *Valdez* ran aground on a reef off Alaska's Prince William Sound, spilling 10 million gallons of oil into the pristine Arctic waters and possibly ruining the area's ecological balance for years to come. An investigation quickly revealed that the *Valdez*'s captain was an unregenerate alcoholic with a long history of drinking on the job. In fact, the accident occurred because he was drunk enough to let an unqualified third mate pilot the giant vessel.

Among other things, the biggest oil spill in U.S. history underscores the need for better applicant and employee testing. Exxon could have saved itself and the environment a lot of grief had it evaluated the captain's alleged sobriety after he underwent treatment for alcoholism.

With substance abuse and employee dishonesty on the rise, employers need to weed out the bad apples before they become problem employees. Unfortunately, Congress is sending out mixed signals about testing and screening.

Drugs and Alcohol

In light of the "just say no" campaign, it's not surprising that Congress and the courts aren't showing much sympathy for job applicants with histories of substance abuse. The move is definitely toward more testing. But even though the courts continue to uphold the legality of drug and alcohol testing, they aren't saying who's responsible for overseeing these testing programs.

Congress wants to shift supervisory responsibility for the administration of drug and alcohol tests from private employers to the Department of Labor. The feeling is that implementing drug and alcohol testing programs isn't a job for amateurs. Like any other growth industry, substance abuse testing has its share of quacks, charlatans, and incompetents. Only standardization and regulation can ensure that substance tests are fair and accurate.

Genetic Testing

In Chapter 5, I explained how some employers are using genetic screening to identify job applicants with a predisposition toward serious illnesses. The practice is becoming particularly widespread in the chemical industry.

At the moment, genetic testing is still legal. But labor unions and liberal legislators view genetic testing as an intrusion into an applicant's privacy and personal life. As the technology for evaluating genetic markers improves, expect more pressure on Congress to regulate genetic testing of applicants and employees.

Background and Credit Checks

Labor and the liberals are also pushing for laws to curb overly zealous employers from probing too deeply into a prospective employee's background. Some employers have gone overboard in their attempts to research applicant records, and there've been serious abuses of privacy. I wouldn't be surprised to see federal and state legislation regulating background checks—not only the way in which employers dig, but what they do with the information once they've dug it up.

Interestingly, Congress is thinking about establishing a Federal Privacy Board similar to those in Europe to regulate the way employers collect, store, and exchange information on current and prospective employees.

The days of using credit information to evaluate job applicants may be numbered. When Congress enacted the Fair Credit Reporting Act, everyone thought the law was going to make it harder for prospective employers and others to abuse credit history information. Not so, apparently, because legislation that would put credit bureaus on an even tighter leash is before Congress now, and a key concern is the use of credit information to screen job applicants.

Many credit records and other personal files are stored in computer databases around the country. Federal and state regulators are concerned about possible employer abuses of this data hoard. Watch for some legal clamps on access to database records.

Lie Detectors and Honesty Tests

Although the Employee Polygraph Protection Act has effectively limited the use of lie detectors in the private sector, new electronic screening devices aimed at getting around present regulations are hitting the market. It's a sure bet, however, that Congress will move quickly to board up any gaps in the present law if it turns out that employers are using these devices to harass or discriminate against job applicants and employees.

Although the polygraph is only marginally useful for determining whether someone is telling the truth, it still has more credibility than the so-called honesty test. The American Psychological Association has even likened honesty testing to voodoo, because its scientific reliability is so suspect.

The lie detector may linger on for a few more years, but honesty testing is definitely on the way out. Several states have already passed laws restricting the use of honesty tests in screening job applicants, and Congress is considering a similar federal law. It looks as if employers will have to find other ways to gauge prospective employees' truthfulness in the future.

Psychological Testing

The psychometric establishment has no quibble with the psychological tests that employers ask applicants to take. Most of them are standard and, if interpreted by a qualified professional, quasi-reliable predictors of behavior.

But not even the most dogged psychometrist can deny that many standard tests (particularly IQ tests) tend to favor the kinds of answers given by white, middle-class respondents. Minority groups have begun to question the usefulness of psychological tests and to point out their potential for abuse. Congress is listening, so we should see efforts to regulate psychological tests, particularly those that might offend groups protected under Title VII.

OTHER TRENDS

Enforcement of laws related to hiring depends partly on who the president appoints to head the Equal Employment Opportunity Commission, the Occupational Safety and Health Administration, and other regulatory bodies. But even when the faces have changed, many of the issues will remain the same.

One of the hottest workplace issues these days is "sick building syndrome." At the Environmental Protection Agency in Washington, D.C., some employers wear respirators to avoid breathing the toxins in the ventilation system and the noxious fumes from the chemicals used to treat the carpets. The developing federal consensus is that all workplaces should be free from hazards, not just the traditionally dangerous ones. Expect the regulators to go for anything that forces employers to eliminate workplace hazards.

Also, several states have enacted laws to protect employees who blow the whistle on employer wrongdoing, and it looks as if Congress will follow suit to protect these informants against vindictive former employers. Expect a lot more legislative action in this arena in the 1990s.

As our society becomes more pluralistic, there are bound to be more legislative attempts to keep the hiring process neutral—more laws, rules, and regulations that you have to deal with every day. But you can do it!

Hiring right isn't all that difficult: Just say tuned in to the law, and don't allow race or sex or religion to interfere with your assessment of an applicant's merit. If you follow these simple guidelines, you'll get the right person for the job without stepping on any legal toes.

INDEX

INS; *see* Immigration and Naturalization Service, The
Institute for the Future, The, 17
Insurance coverage, 156
Interviewing, 90–91
  errors and, 109
  guidelines to questions, 98–99
  legal employer demands, 98
  questions to avoid, 91
  tactics for, 100–101
  traps to avoid, 107
IQ tests, 182
IRCA; *see* Immigration Reform and Control Act of 986, The

J

Job application
  applicant's signature, 42
  content of, 40–43
  general questions on, 41
  screening period, 41–42
Job competition and scams, 49
Job titles and responsibilities, 47–48
Jury duty, 97

K-L

Knowing the applicants, 34
Labor-Management Service Administration, The (LMSA), 122
Language, 105
Laws to know when recruiting, 31
Lie-detector tests, 69, 84–87
  definition, 85
  for internal criminal investigations, 86
  future trends, 181–82
  and state laws, 87
Limited partnerships, 55
Location of employment, 154

M

Marital status, 92
Medical records, 25–26

Merit and qualifications, 15
Military service, 96
Monitoring phone calls, 27
Mothers Against Drunk Driving, 81

N

Name change, 96
National Institute of Alcoholism and Alcohol Abuse, The, 81
National Labor Relations Act, The, 80, 97
National Labor Relations Board, The, 74
New York Business Group on Health, The, 83
Noncompetition agreements, 157–58
"Non-spousal rule," 103

O

Occupational Safety and Health Act of 1970, The (OSHA), 70–71
Occupational Safety and Health Administration, The, 120
Occupational Safety and Health Review Commission, The 121
OFCCP; *see* Office of Federal Contract Compliance Programs, The
Office of Administrative Law Judges, 118–19
Office of Federal Contract Compliance Programs, The 10–11, 37, 111, 119–20
Office of Special Counsel in the Department of Justice, The, 59–60
Omissions, 108
Opinion Research Corp., 46
Ownership of work product, 156–57

P

"Paper polygraphs;" *see* Honesty tests
Partners, 35
Personal finances, 95